GRADE 3

Challenging Common Core Math Lessons

ACTIVITIES AND EXTENSIONS FOR GIFTED AND ADVANCED LEARNERS IN

GRADE 3

Challenging Common Core Math Lessons

MARGARET JESS MCKOWEN PATTI

CENTER FOR GIFTED EDUCATION

P.O. Box 8795
Williamsburg, VA 23187

Edited by Lacy Compton

Cover design by Raquel Trevino and layout design by Allegra Denbo

ISBN-13: 978-1-61821-410-2

At the time of this book's publication, all facts and figures cited are the most current available; all telephone numbers, addresses, and website URLs are accurate and active; all publications, organizations, websites, and other resources exist as described in this book; and all have been verified. The author and Prufrock Press make no warranty or guarantee concerning the information and materials given out by organizations or content found at websites, and we are not responsible for any changes that occur after this book's publication. If you find an error or believe that a resource listed here is not as described, please contact Prufrock Press.

Prufrock Press Inc.
P.O. Box 8813
Waco, TX 76714-8813
Phone: (800) 998-2208
Fax: (800) 240-0333
http://www.prufrock.com

TABLE OF CONTENTS

INTRODUCTION

The Common Core State Standards (CCSS) for Mathematics are K–12 curriculum standards that describe the mathematics skills and concepts students need to develop for success in higher education and the 21st-century workplace. The CCSS for Mathematics consists of two parts:

- The Standards for Mathematical Content, which define what students should understand and be able to do in their study of mathematics. The content standards balance procedure and understanding.
- The Standards for Mathematical Practice, which describe ways to process and show proficiency when engaging with a mathematical concept.

With the adoption of the CCSS in nearly every state, gifted and advanced learners need opportunities to master grade-level standards and mathematical practices with greater depth, rigor, and understanding. This book is one of a series of books developed in conjunction with the Center for Gifted Education at William & Mary intended to give gifted and advanced learners additional practice and activities to master and engage with the CCSS for Mathematics. Each book in the series is organized by the content standards in one grade.

The lessons in this book cover Grade 3 mathematics content. In Grade 3, the standards are addressed in five domains:

- Operations and Algebraic Thinking,
- Number and Operations in Base Ten,
- Number and Operations—Fractions,
- Measurement and Data, and
- Geometry.

STANDARDS FOR MATHEMATICAL PRACTICE

To engage learners with the Standards for Mathematical Content, the CCSS describe the Standards for Mathematical Practice—ways to connect with the content standards at every grade level:

1. Make sense of problems and persevere in solving them.
2. Reason abstractly and quantitatively.
3. Construct viable arguments and critique the reasoning of others.
4. Model with mathematics.
5. Use appropriate tools strategically.

6. Attend to precision.
7. Look for and make use of structure.
8. Look for and express regularity in repeated reasoning.

Each lesson in this book identifies the mathematical practices by number. Activities and practice problems are structured to develop mathematical practices in learners. Teachers should be aware of the practices and look for opportunities to connect mathematical practices to content understanding in every lesson.

PURPOSE

The lessons in this book were written with the assumption that a teacher has already introduced a mathematical content standard through a primary curriculum source. Problem solving, practice problems, and activities enrich and extend current grade-level mathematics content rather than accelerate students to above-grade-level content. Each lesson is specific to a standard, usually only focusing on one or two content standards, and provides additional support and enrichment for gifted and advanced learners.

LESSON STRUCTURE

Each lesson follows a predictable structure. It first begins by naming the focal standard(s)—what students should already know or to which they have been introduced. Next, the Standards for Mathematical Practice covered within the activities and problems are listed by number. The lesson includes an estimate for the time it might take to complete the lesson; however, this will vary by teacher and classroom. Key terms are listed, and are included based on when the terms are first introduced in the CCSS or are a prerequisite for understanding the activity or problems in a lesson. Teachers should be sure their students already have a working knowledge of these terms before beginning the lesson.

Every lesson includes a list of materials needed, including handouts. It is assumed that students will have access to commonplace items such as pencils and paper, and the materials noted are those items that teachers will need to obtain/acquire in advance. The lesson objectives highlight what students will learn or be able to do as a result of completing the activities and problems.

All lessons include an opening activity to allow students to explore the concept (e.g., multiple representations, open-ended problems, observing number patterns). Each activity is followed by practice problems that challenge students (e.g., harder or less familiar numbers) and—more importantly—extend students' thinking beyond calculating an answer. The practice problems ask students to grapple with their understanding of the lesson concepts. The lessons conclude with an assessment practice that allows teachers to evaluate student learning. The practice problems were written to engage gifted and advanced learners in higher level thinking and deeper understanding of a mathematical concept. The Common Core Assessment Practice problems in this book were intentionally written for students to practice and prepare for on-level standardized test questions similar to CCSS-based grade-level assessments, given all students are required to take these types of assessments.

GROUPING OPTIONS

The lessons in this book can be used for whole-group, small-group, and individual instruction.

Whole-Group Instruction

Teachers can use this book in one academic year in conjunction with the primary curriculum in a gifted or advanced mathematics class. All students would complete each lesson after being introduced to a particular content standard. Teachers can integrate the lessons into the primary curriculum taught to a whole group and address higher order thinking questions through the lesson activity and practice problems.

Small-Group Instruction

Teachers can use this book to differentiate learning in any mathematics class by creating flexible student groups and giving students who need enrichment an opportunity for deeper understanding and engagement with a concept. Students can complete activities and practice at a self-guided pace with a partner or small group and engage in peer discussion, with or without directed supervision or intervention from the teacher.

Individual Instruction

The practice problems and assessment questions in each lesson are a good way to determine individual understanding of a certain mathematics concept on a deeper level. Nearly every practice problem emphasizes making sense of and communicating the process of problem solving and asks students to explain their thinking.

SECTION I

Number and Operations in Base Ten

LESSON 1.1

Addition and Subtraction With Place Value and Rounding

Common Core State Standards

- 3.NBT.1
- 3.NBT.2

Mathematical Practices

- 2, 3, 4, 5, and 6

Estimated Time

- 60 minutes

Key Terms

- Precise
- Estimate
- Addends

Materials

- Lesson 1.1 Activity: Budget Plans for Businesses
- Lesson 1.1 Practice: Place Value and Rounding
- Lesson 1.1 Common Core Assessment Practice

Objectives

In this lesson, students will:

- formulate a budget plan using place value and rounding,
- explain the relationship between two expressions using properties of multiplication, and
- model rounding of numbers on a number line.

Lesson 1.1 Activity: Budget Plans for Businesses

In this activity, students will work in pairs to develop a business plan. Students will be asked to start a business for the local outdoor community market day where various vendors sell their items. To begin, students will formulate a budget plan that meets the given requirements. Each business is loaned $350 and must choose three start-up items to purchase from a list of items. Students will determine the precise amount of money spent, the precise amount of money left over, and an estimate of how much money would be needed to purchase all of the start-up items on the list. Students will also explain the relationship between two different business scenarios, making the connection to properties of addition and subtraction. Students will represent the rounding of numbers within their businesses on a number line.

NAME:______________________________ DATE:______________

LESSON 1.1 ACTIVITY

Budget Plans for Businesses

Directions: Complete the steps below.

Today, you will work with a partner to decide on a business idea and business name for an outdoor community market day. It is now time to begin your business plans. Remember, a business always wants to pay off any debt first, and then make a profit. Wise decisions are a must! Who is up for the challenge? Fill in your business name and type on the lines below.

Name of Business:______________________________

Type of Business:______________________________

Businesses will be loaned $350 for start-up costs. Take a look at the table below, which displays the necessities your business can purchase, and decide on the three most important necessities to buy.

Necessities	Cost
Table for displaying items	$119
Sign for advertising	$43
Items to sell	$87
Employee to work the table	$122
Cash register	$24
Tent to provide shade	$58

Write the three start-up necessities in the space below.

1. ______________________________

____

2. ______________________________

____

3. ______________________________

____

Once you have decided which three necessities will be purchased, discuss the following questions with your partner and write a response to each.

1. You were told to choose three necessities to purchase.
   a. How much money did your business spend on the three necessities? ________
   b. How many hundreds? ________
   c. How many tens? ________
   d. How many ones? ________

2. How much money do you have left for additional purchases?
   a. How many hundreds? ________
   b. How many tens? ________
   c. How many ones? ________

3. About how much money would you need to purchase all of the necessities listed in the table? ________ Explain how you developed your estimate.

4. Suppose you and your partner decided to purchase a sign and table for your new business. A few days later, you realize it is supposed to rain on the day of the outdoor market, so you use some of your remaining start-up money to purchase a tent.
   a. How much money did you and your partner spend? ________ Write a number sentence to show your purchases.
   b. Now, suppose a competing business purchased a tent and a sign, but a few days later, its owners decide they also needed a table to display their product. How much money did the competing business spend? ________ Write a number sentence to show its purchases.
   c. Explain how the sums in Parts A and B are equal using the associative property.

5. You and your partner disagree on how to estimate for the total cost of all of necessities on the list.
   a. When estimating the total of all necessities, your partner says that the price of the table, which is $119, should be rounded to $100. You disagree and say that the price of the table should be rounded to $120. What can you infer about each business partner's approach to the estimation?
   b. Model your partner's approach to the problem by using the number line provided to round.

   c. Model your approach to the problem by using the provided number line provided to round.

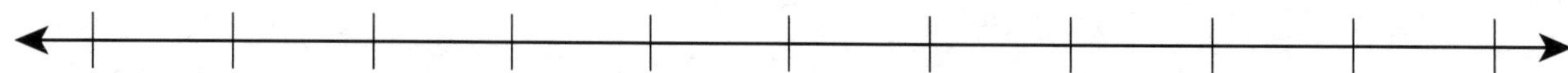

Extend Your Thinking

1. If you were loaned $420, what additional necessities could you have purchased for your business along with the three you originally chose?

2. Now that you have started your business, it is time to determine what you will sell at the outdoor market in your local community. Think about items that people would likely purchase while walking around a market. List three items that you plan to sell and decide how much you will charge for each item. How should you use the start-up cost in the calculation? Explain why you chose each price for your three items and how your decision is related to the start-up cost.

NAME:______________________________ DATE:______________

LESSON 1.1 PRACTICE

Place Value and Rounding

Directions: Complete the problems below.

1. Demetria is bringing candy as a surprise to all 396 kids in her school. Demetria would like for each student to receive one piece of candy. The candy is sold in bags of 50 pieces per bag. How should she determine the number of bags of candy to buy? Justify your answer by providing proof.

2. Compose a word problem in which estimation would be the best method to solve.

3. Compose a word problem in which a precise answer would be the best method to solve.

4. What is 12.6 rounded to the nearest whole number? ________

5. Using the digits 6, 7, 8, and 9, complete each number sentence. A digit can only be used once in each number sentence.

   a. ____ ____ + ____ ____ = 147

   b. ____ ____ + ____ ____ = 174

   c. ____ ____ + ____ ____ = 165

6. Is there any other way to arrange the digits in Question 5C and still get a sum of 165? Explain your answer.

7. Read the clues below.

I composed three hundreds out of 30 tens and had 2 tens left over.
I didn't need to compose any additional tens because all I had were 5 ones.

a. What number is being described? ________
b. Round the number being described to the nearest ten and then subtract it from 500. What is the difference? ________

8. Read the clues below.

2 thousands	21 hundreds	9 tens	4 ones

a. What number is being described? ________
b. Round the number being described to the nearest hundred and then subtract it from 5,000. What is the difference? ________

9. Read the clues below.

1 hundreds	28 tens	5 ones

a. What number is being described? ________

10. Rebekah has saved 2,654 pennies. Claudia has saved 169 pennies.
a. About how many pennies does Rebekah have saved? ________
b. About how many pennies does Claudia have saved? ________
c. Precisely how many more pennies do Rebekah and Claudia need in order to reach a total of 3,000 pennies? ________

Extend Your Thinking

1. Problem 5 required you to determine the missing numbers. How does looking at the sum help you strategically place the digits?

2. Create a place value question. Give a peer any four digits to arrange to get a specific sum. Use the above problems as a guide to creating your question, and be sure to include an answer key.

NAME: ____________________ DATE: __________

LESSON 1.1

Common Core Assessment Practice

1. On Monday, José spent 27 minutes on math homework, and he read for 43 minutes. He spent the exact same time on math and reading during Tuesday night's homework as he did on Monday night.
   a. Round the time to get an estimate on the number of minutes José spent on homework for Monday night and Tuesday night all together.

   b. About how many hours did José spend? ________

2. Kendrick said that he had 177 more tickets for the school fair than his friend Tommy, who only had 81 tickets.
   a. How many tickets did Kendrick have for the school fair? ________
   b. About how many tickets did Kendrick and Tommy have all together? Round the numbers to get an estimated answer. ________

   c. The oversized stuffed giraffe at the fair requires 159 more tickets than Kendrick currently has saved. How many tickets does it take to purchase the giraffe? _____

   d. If Tommy gives Kendrick all of his tickets, how many more tickets would Kendrick still have to save to purchase the giraffe? ________

3. On Saturday, two basketball teams played against each other. The winning team scored 40 points during the game, and the losing team scored 23 points.
   a. How many more points did the winning team score than the losing team? ______

   b. Estimate how many total points were scored during the basketball game. ______

LESSON 1.2

Using Place Value to Multiply

Common Core State Standards

- 3.NBT.3

Mathematical Practices

- 2, 3, 6, 7, and 8

Estimated Time

- 60 minutes

Key Terms

- Product
- Multiple of ten
- Factor
- Standard form
- Compose

Materials

- Lesson 1.2 Activity: Mind Readers
- Lesson 1.2: Mind Readers Chart Player A
- Lesson 1.2: Mind Readers Chart Player B
- Lesson 1.2 Practice: Using Place Value
- Lesson 1.2 Common Core Assessment Practice

Objectives

In this lesson, students will:

- employ efficient strategies to multiply numbers by multiples of ten based on place value and properties of operations,
- solve multiplication problems based on the concept of place value, and
- generate place value explanations for products of devised multiplication problems.

Lesson 1.2 Activity: Mind Readers

In this activity, students will work in pairs to play Mind Readers. Each student needs a Mind Readers Chart to record his or her thoughts and answers separately. Player A will think of a multiplication problem. One factor, or number that is being multiplied, should be a two-digit multiple of 10. The other factor should be a one-digit number. For example, Player A might mentally create the multiplication problem 60×6. The expression meets the criteria because 60 is a two-digit multiple of 10 and 6 is a one-digit number. Player A should not tell his or her partner the multiplication problem, but instead should describe the product, or answer to the multiplication problem, in place value terms. To describe the product of the example, Player A could say, "The product is 36 tens." Player A would then secretly determine all of the various factors that could have been used to get the result of 36 tens and record it on the Mind Readers Chart.

Player B needs to think about the product and decide how 36 tens would be written in standard form (360). Knowing that one of the factors has to be a multiple of 10 and the other a one-digit number, Player B must utilize prior knowledge that 6 × 6 equals 36, and therefore 60 × 6 = 360. Student B should try to determine every multiplication fact that follows the guidelines and has a product of 360. After Player B reveals what he or she believes to be the multiplication problems resulting in the described product, the student pair needs to discuss any problems that do not match. Students should determine how many possible multiplication problems Player A could have created with the specified product. Students will switch roles after each round. Players A and B should fill in their Mind Readers Chart as the game is played.

NAME:____ DATE:______________

LESSON 1.2 ACTIVITY

Mind Readers

Directions: It is time to use your mathematical mind to determine what your partner is thinking! Work with a partner to play Mind Readers. Decide who will be Player A and who will be Player B.

1. Player A: Think of a secret multiplication problem that follows these rules: One factor must be a two-digit multiple of 10 and the other factor must be a one-digit number. For example, $60 \times 4 = 240$.

2. Player A: Solve your secret multiplication problem using place value knowledge. Record your secret multiplication problem on your Mind Readers Chart. Next, describe the product using place value terms to your partner. Record your description on the chart. For example, to describe 240, you could say, "Twenty-four tens."

3. Student B: Write the number that is being described using place value terms in standard form. Record the standard form of the number on your Mind Readers chart. Use the description of the product to determine the possible secret multiplication problems. Student B should remember:
   - One factor had to be a two-digit multiple of 10.
   - One factor had to be a one-digit number.

4. Student B: You are also determining all of the different factors your partner could have thought of based on the described product. If you and your partner disagree with the multiplication problems, you must discuss if an error was made, or if there was more than one possible answer.

5. Once Student B gets the correct multiplication problem, switch roles.

After playing the game, discuss the following and respond.

1. Think about the practice problems you completed while playing the game. What patterns do you recognize?

2. Discuss and explain why you believe some numbers had more than one correct multiplication sentence that could result with the same product.

Extend Your Thinking

1. Play Mind Readers using new rules. One factor must be a three-digit multiple of 10, and the other factor must be a two- or three-digit number.

2. Explain how you are able to solve the problems by drawing Base Ten blocks to demonstrate the place value relationship.

NAME:______________________ DATE:__________

LESSON 1.2

Mind Readers Chart

PLAYER A

Round 1 Player A

Secret Multiplication Problem	Standard Form	Describe Product in Place Value Terms	Possible Factors That Could Result in the Product

Round 2 Player A

Secret Multiplication Problem	Standard Form	Describe Product in Place Value Terms	Possible Factors That Could Result in the Product

Round 3 Player A

Secret Multiplication Problem	Standard Form	Describe Product in Place Value Terms	Possible Factors That Could Result in the Product

NAME:______________________________ DATE:______________

LESSON 1.2

Mind Readers Chart

PLAYER B

Round 1 Player B

Secret Multiplication Problem	Standard Form	Describe Product in Place Value Terms	Possible Factors That Could Result in the Product

Round 2 Player B

Secret Multiplication Problem	Standard Form	Describe Product in Place Value Terms	Possible Factors That Could Result in the Product

Round 3 Player B

Secret Multiplication Problem	Standard Form	Describe Product in Place Value Terms	Possible Factors That Could Result in the Product

NAME:______________________________ DATE:______________

LESSON 1.2 PRACTICE

Using Place Value

Directions: Complete the problems below.

1. The following problem is missing two factors. You know one factor is a two-digit multiple of 10, and the other is a one-digit number.
   a. What are the missing factors? ________ × ________ = 560

   b. Are those the only possible factors? Explain.

2. While playing Mind Readers, two students disagreed on the multiplication problems that had a product of 36 tens. Player A said that 60 × 6 equals 36 tens, but Player B said that 4 × 90 equals 36 tens.
   a. Who do you agree with and why?

   b. Come up with another way to write 36 tens as a product.

3. While playing Mind Readers, two players disagreed on the multiplication problem. Student 1 said that the problem should have read 40 × 5 = 200, and Student 2 said that the problem should have read 50 × 4 = 200.
   a. Which student is correct? ________

   b. How do you know?

4. $5 \times 3 =$ ________ ones. Therefore, 50, or 5 ________ times $3 = 150$ ones or 15 ________.

5. Explain the difference between 30×7 and 300×7.

Extend Your Thinking

1. Multiply by multiples of 100 to determine products using place value knowledge.

2. Demonstrate each explanation using Base Ten blocks.

NAME:____ DATE:__________________

LESSON 1.2

Common Core Assessment Practice

1. Explain how knowing the product of 3 × 8 will help you solve for the product of 3 × 80 and 8 × 30.

2. The product of 60 × 2 is 12 tens. Write 12 tens in standard form.

3. Knowing the product of 60 × 2 should help you determine the product of 6 × 2, which equals ________ ones, and 6 × 20, which equals ________ tens.

4. Nehemiah says that 70 × 5 is 350 because 7 × 5 is 35, so you can just add a zero. Explain the reason behind adding the zero.

5. What is the product of 40 × 5?

SECTION II

Operations and Algebraic Thinking

LESSON 2.1

Meaning and Strategies of Multiplication

Common Core State Standards

- 3.OA.1
- 3.OA.5

Mathematical Practices

- 1, 2, 3, 4, 6, 7, and 8

Estimated Time

- 60 minutes

Key Terms

- Decompose

Materials

- Lesson 2.1 Activity: Proper Placement of Properties
- Lesson 2.1 Scenario Cards
- Lesson 2.1 Practice: Multiplication
- Lesson 2.1 Common Core Assessment Practice
- Bag for cards

Objectives

In this lesson, students will:

- categorize various scenarios based on knowledge of properties of multiplication,
- support categorizing decisions with mathematical explanations,
- calculate to determine products, and
- assess strategies involving properties of operations to multiply and divide.

Lesson 2.1 Activity: Proper Placement of Properties

In this activity, students will work in small groups to solve various scenarios and determine which property of multiplication is being described. Students need to be able to write on the scenario cards to solve and respond to questions. Teachers should place the cutout cards in a bag along with the sheet and provide one bag for each group. Students will draw one card at a time, discuss and solve the problem on the card, and then categorize the card based on the property of multiplication to which it relates.

NAME:________________________________ DATE:______________

LESSON 2.1 ACTIVITY

Proper Placement of Properties

Directions: Pull one scenario card at a time out of the bag. With your group, discuss and solve the problem on the card. Then, categorize the card into one of the five properties of multiplication. Repeat these steps until all of the cards have been discussed, solved, and placed into a category.

Extend Your Thinking

1. Could any of the scenario cards have been placed in more than one group? Explain your answer.

2. Determine if any properties of multiplication are also true for division. Think about the meaning of each property and apply it to a few division problems.

NAME:______________________________ DATE:______________

LESSON 2.1

Scenario Cards

1. Sammy made two 6 by 7 arrays and said $(6 \times 7) + (6 \times 7)$ was equal to $2(6 \times 7)$. Do you agree with Sammy? Explain why or why not. Explain to Sammy that to solve $2 \times 6 \times 7$, he could have also made 7 different arrays, each representing the multiplication facts _____ × _____.	**2.** Carolina does not know the product of 12×11. She was told to decompose the 11 into 10 and 1, and then find the sum of 12 times 10 and 12 times 1. Write the expression that is described. Suggest another way to decompose 11 that would help Carolina multiply 12 times 11.
3. Knowing that 17×2 equals 34 can help Aaron solve 17×4 because he could decompose the 4 into _____ + _____. Write an equation that represents the equivalence of 17×4 and the decomposed expression.	**4.** Sue attempted to shoot the basketball into the net seven times on Monday, seven times on Tuesday, and seven times on Wednesday. She was unsuccessful with every attempt and described her experience as _____ shots with zero accuracy ($21 \times 0 = 0$). Her coach said she should think of it as 0 successful attempts for _____ shots equals 0 points. Who is correct, Sue or her coach? Explain your answer.

Operations and Algebraic Thinking

Operations and Algebraic Thinking

5. When given six arrays, George took notes to help him discover a pattern, but he couldn't determine the rule for the pattern. Use the notes to explain to George the rule that supports this pattern.

Array	Number of Rows	Number in Each Row	Product
A	7	1	7
B	27	1	27
C	1	54	54
D	1	12	12
E	19	1	19
F	81	1	81

6. Chastity is trying to determine the value of the variable N in the problem $(8 \times 6) + (N \times 4) = 80$. She knows that $8 \times 6 = 48$. Chastity also knows that $80 - 48 = 32$. How can this help her determine the variable N?

7. In our numeral system, we have a unique number. No matter what you multiply this number by, it will always equal itself. What number is being described?

Can you think of any other unique numbers in our numeral system?

8. Draw two arrays to prove that the order in which the factors are multiplied does not affect the product. Use the product of 60.

- How many groups are in your first array?
- What is the size of each group in your first array?
- How many groups are in your second array?
- What is the size of each group in your second array?

9. Will zero groups of five have the same product as seven groups of zero? Explain your answer using number sentences or word sentences.	**10.** Rafael informed his teacher that he knew the product of 5 × 10 as well as the product of 5 × 6, but he didn't know the product of 16 × 5. The teacher told him to apply the facts he knew to solve the unknown multiplication product. How can Rafael use the two multiplication problems to determine the product of 16 × 5? Solve the problem.
11. Tamika knows all of the 3 multiplication facts from zero to 12, so therefore she knows that 3 × 6 = 18. When asked to solve 6 × 3, Tamika said she wasn't sure of the answer because she hasn't learned her 6 multiplication facts. Explain to Tamika that she does know what 6 × 3 is based on her knowledge of 3 × 6 equaling 18.	**12.** You are at a math contest, and you can only use numbers and signs, including =, ( ), +, –, ÷, and ×, to prove your thoughts. Following the contest rules, show that the way in which factors are grouped when being multiplied won't affect the product. Show this with the numbers 7, 8, and 9.

13. $14 \times 4 = 56$ and $14 \times 7 = 98$. Therefore, $14(4 + 7) =$ ____ + ____ = ____.	**14.** Laverne is trying to utilize a property of multiplication to help her solve 212×15. Laverne was informed that she could solve the problem in two different ways. Help her by filling in the blanks. $(212 \times 15) = (212 \times$ ___$) +$ $(212 \times$ ___$)$ or $($____$\times 15) + ($____$\times 15)$. Are these the only two ways that Laverne could use to help her solve 212×15? If not, how else could she have reached the product?

NAME:____ DATE:________________

LESSON 2.1 PRACTICE

Multiplication

Directions: Complete the problems below.

1. Find the products below. What appears to be true about the order in which you multiply numbers? Prove your generalization by writing a problem to test your answer.

   a. $19 \times 8 =$ ______

   $8 \times 19 =$ ______

   b. $23 \times 7 =$ ______

   $7 \times 23 =$ ______

2. How could the fact that $7 \times 8 = 56$ and $2 \times 8 = 16$ help you calculate the product of 9×8?

3. Create the following word problems.

   a. Create a word problem that represents seven groups with 12 objects in each group.

   b. Create a word problem that represents 12 groups with seven objects in each.

c. What do you notice about Questions 3A and 3B? How is this related to the work you did in Question 1? How do you know?

4. $(7 \times 5) \times 2$ equals $7 \times (5 \times 2)$ but $(20 - 10) - 5$ does not equal $20 - (10 - 5)$. What can you conclude about the associative property based on this knowledge?

5. The school bought 6 boxes of red markers and 4 boxes of blue markers. If each box has 9 markers, how many markers did the school order in all? Show the product in two different ways using numbers, pictures, or words.

Extend Your Thinking

1. Create an example of a multiplication problem that is related to at least two properties of multiplication.

NAME:______________________________ DATE:______________

LESSON 2.1

Common Core Assessment Practice

Directions: Complete the problems below.

1. Which is the correct expression that describes the following array? Explain your reasoning.

   x x x x x
   x x x x x
   x x x x x

   a. 15×3
   b. 3×5
   c. 15×5
   d. $3 + 3$

2. Circle all that describe the following expression: 9×8.
   a. William had nine problems that each had eight steps to solve.
   b. William added nine 8 times.
   c. William had nine groups with eight in each.
   d. William had an array with nine rows of eight apples.

3. Mary Beth earns $8 every week that she weeds and waters the flower beds in her neighborhood. She does the work for 7 weeks. How much money does Mary Beth make weeding and watering the flowerbeds?
   a. $48
   b. $64
   c. $49
   d. $56

4. Which property of multiplication is being modeled in the following expression: $6 \times (4 + 3) = 6 \times 4 + 6 \times 3$
   a. Associative property of multiplication
   b. Distributive property of multiplication
   c. Identity property of multiplication
   d. Multiplicative property of one

5. Which of the following is not equivalent to $6 \times 13 \times 5$? What is wrong with the incorrect expression?
   a. $(6 \times 13)5$
   b. $(5 \times 13)6$
   c. 5×18
   d. $13(5 \times 6)$

LESSON 2.2

Meaning and Strategies of Division

Common Core State Standards

- 3.OA.2
- 3.OA.6

Mathematical Practices

- 1, 2, 3, 4, 5, 6, 7, and 8

Estimated Time

- 60 minutes

Key Terms

- Fact family

Materials

- Lesson 2.2 Activity: Multiply to Divide
- Lesson 2.2 Fact Families
- Lesson 2.2 Number Cards
- Lesson 2.2 Practice: Division
- Lesson 2.2 Common Core Assessment Practice
- Bag for cards
- Glue sticks

Objectives

In this lesson, students will:

- represent division as an unknown factor problem,
- recognize that multiplication and division are inverse operations, and
- calculate to determine quotients.

Lesson 2.2 Activity: Multiply to Divide

In this activity, students will work in pairs to create multiplication and division fact families. The number cards need to be cut out and placed in a bag for each group. Students will then take all of the numbers out of the bag and lay them face up so each student in the pair can see all of the numbers. Students will work together to choose three numbers that can be used to create a multiplication and division fact family. Students will place those three numbers in one box on the activity sheet. All numbers must be used. In the event that the last three numbers will not create a fact family, students must problem solve to see which fact family can be changed so that all numbers are used to create correct families.

NAME:______________________________ DATE:______________

LESSON 2.2 ACTIVITY

Multiply to Divide

Directions: With a partner, pull out all of the numbers and place them face up. Choose three numbers that will create a multiplication and division fact family. Lay the three numbers on the activity sheet, but do not glue the numbers yet.

Keep choosing three numbers at a time to create a fact family and place them on the activity sheet. If you get to the last three numbers, and they don't create a fact family, discuss how you can make changes so all of the numbers make fact families. All numbers must be used. Once you agree on the placement of all of the numbers, glue the numbers to the paper.

Extend Your Thinking

1. Think of a number that could create at least two different fact families.

NAME:____________________ DATE:__________

LESSON 2.2

Fact Families

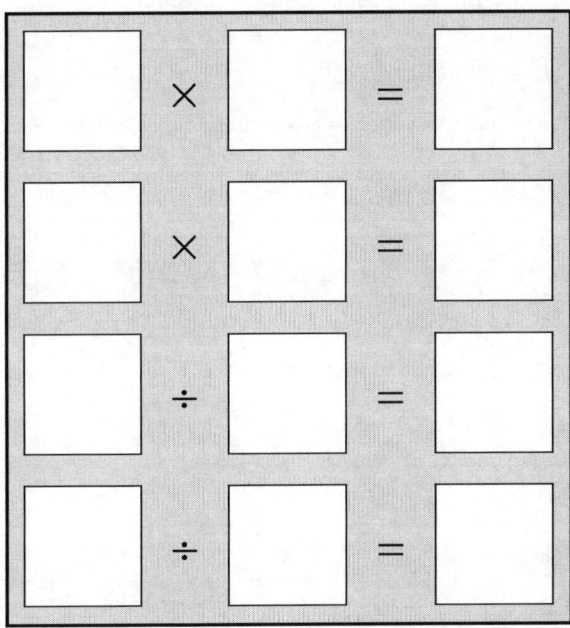

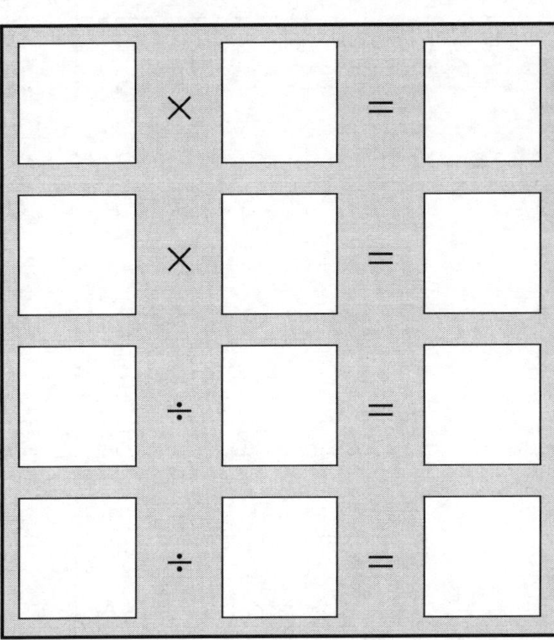

NAME:________________________________ DATE:____________

LESSON 2.2

Number Cards

8	10	4	7	32	70
16	2	4	9	4	18
36	36	6	6	6	6
15	70	3	10	5	7
18	18	9	2	2	9
7	16	10	4	70	4
32	15	4	5	8	3
6	70	6	7	36	10
5	32	3	8	15	4
36	18	6	9	6	2
4	32	4	8	16	4
16	3	4	5	4	15

NAME:______________________________ DATE:______________

LESSON 2.2 PRACTICE

Division

Directions: Complete the problems below.

1. Because you know 16 × 7, or 16 groups of 7, equals 112, you also know that 112 has how many groups of 16? Show your answer using a number bond.

2. There are many different fact families that can be used to represent the number 32. The number 16 can be multiplied by _______, and the number 8 can be multiplied by _______. Therefore, you know that 32 can be divided evenly by what numbers? Write the fact families you used to arrive at your answer.

3. Draw an array and write a multiplication equation to represent 54 divided into nine groups. How many are in each group? _______

4. Two hundred and twenty-five Skittles are divided into equal groups.
   a. Suppose you divide the number of Skittles equally among 25 students in your class. How many Skittles does each person get? ________

   b. Divide 225 into a different number of groups than in Part A. How many groups did you divide 225 into? ________ What was the size of the groups? ________ What is a multiplication equation you could use to represent your problem? ________________________ Write a related division equation. ________________________

   c. What is another way to divide the Skittles evenly?

   d. Suppose your teacher would like to have some Skittles also, meaning you need to divide the 225 Skittles into 26 groups. How should you do this?

5. How many times can you subtract 11 from 110? Write the related division equation.

6. Solve for the missing factor, and then write the related division equation.

   a. $4 \times$ ________ $= 28$

   b. ________ $\times 12 = 36$

   c. $18 =$ ________ $\times 6$

   d. What can you infer about the numbers 36 and 18 from Parts B and C based on the missing factor of each problem? Give another example of a number that fits this pattern.

NAME:________________________ DATE:____________

LESSON 2.2

Common Core Assessment Practice

Directions: Complete the problems below.

1. Raphael has 24 flowers to distribute evenly among 4 flower arrangements. How many flowers will be in each arrangement? ________ Which expression represents the above problem? How do you know?

   a. $24 \times 4 =$ ________

   b. $4 \times 24 =$ ________

   c. $24 \div 4 =$ ________

   d. $4 \div 24 =$ ________

2. A grocery store has 21 canned goods that need to be placed evenly on the shelves. There are a total of 3 shelves. How many canned goods should be placed on each shelf? ________ Circle all of the expressions that can be used to solve the above problem. Explain your reasoning.

   a. $3 \div 21 =$ ________

   b. $3 \times n = 21$

   c. $21 \div 3 =$ ________

   d. $3 \div n = 21$

3. Which expression could be used to help you solve $64 \div 8$? How could this expression help you?
   a. $8 \times N$
   b. 64×8
   c. 8×64
   d. $8 \div 64$

Operations and Algebraic Thinking

4. Solve for the unknown: $30 \div 6 = N$. Circle your answer below. Draw a picture to show how you arrived at your answer.
   a. $N = 180$
   b. $N = 6$
   c. $N = 36$
   d. $N = 5$

5. Which equation could help you solve for the unknown factor in $8 \times P = 32$? How would you use the equation?
   a. $32 \times 8 = P$
   b. $8 \times 32 = P$
   c. $P = 32 \div 8$
   d. $P = 8 \div 32$

6. Peter says that 108 can be divided into 9 equal groups. Kayla says that 108 can be divided into 2 equal groups. Which student is correct? How do you know?

LESSON 2.3

Relationship Between Multiplication and Division

Common Core State Standards

- 3.OA.4
- 3.OA.6
- 3.OA.7

Mathematical Practices

- 1, 2, 6, 7, and 8

Estimated Time

- 60 minutes

Key Terms

- Equation
- Expression

Materials

- Lesson 2.3 Activity: Make the Match
- Lesson 2.3 Equations/Answer Sheet
- Lesson 2.3 Recording Sheet: Distributive Property
- Lesson 2.3 Recording Sheet: Commutative Property
- Lesson 2.3 Recording Sheet: Associative Property
- Lesson 2.3 Recording Sheet: Inverse Operations
- Lesson 2.3 Recording Sheet: Strategies and Additional Problems
- Lesson 2.3 Practice: Multiplication and Division
- Lesson 2.3 Common Core Assessment Practice
- Bag for cards
- Glue sticks

Objectives

In this lesson, students will:

- discover the relationship between multiplication and division,
- reorganize expressions based on equivalence, and
- utilize various strategies to solve problems.

Lesson 2.3 Activity: Make the Match

Prior to this activity, teachers should review the properties of multiplication and how they help students solve problems for which the facts aren't memorized. Students probably don't have 98×3 memorized, but they can determine the product by using the distributive property; for example: $98 \times 3 = (90 + 8) \times 3$. Students know $90 \times 3 = 270$ and $8 \times 3 = 24$, so $270 + 24 = 294$.

Students will work in pairs to play a game of memory. Each expression has a matching expression that is equivalent, but is solved using a different strategy. Students will turn over one expression at a time and then try to find its matching pair. If the student fails to make a match, the next player will take a turn. If the student does make a match, he or she proves the expressions are equivalent by working the problem while the other student checks over the work. Once a match is made, the two students will work together to determine which property was used on the matching cards. The students will then glue the two expressions to the corresponding properties sheet to make an equation. If the problems do not pertain to a property, students will simply glue them on the Strategies and Additional Problems recording sheet.

NAME: ____________________ DATE: ____________

LESSON 2.3 ACTIVITY

Make the Match

Directions: It's time to test your memory skills as well as your knowledge of properties. Be ready to take a picture with your mind of various expressions. With a partner, pull all of the expressions out of the bag and place them face down in front of you. Play memory by choosing two expressions that are equivalent and can be joined to create an equation. Matches will be based on properties and strategies you have learned.

Continue matching the expressions based on properties and strategies until all of the equations have been created. Prove the expressions are equivalent by solving each side of the problems. Glue each equation to the corresponding recording sheet based on the represented property or strategy. Be sure to check the work of your partner as he or she is working.

Extend Your Thinking

1. Look at the division expressions. The original division problem has been broken into two smaller division problems. With your partner, decide if the problem could have been broken up into any other combinations and record those on your sheet.

2. Use the equations on the Distributive Property recording sheet to help you solve the following question: How could the fact that $10 - 1 = 9$ help you solve 9×25?

NAME:______________________________ DATE:______________

LESSON 2.3

Equations/Answer Sheet

$(11 \times 2) + (11 \times 10)$	11×12
$64 \div 8$	$8 \times n = 64$
25×7	$(20 + 5) \times 7$
45×4	4×45
$48 \div 6$	$(30 \div 6) + (18 \div 6)$
$9 \times 6 \times 7$	$(9 \times 6)7$ or $(6 \times 7)9$ or $(7 \times 9)6$
$6(7 + 8)$	$(6 \times 7) + (6 \times 8)$
$4 \times 3 \times 6$	$(4 \times 3)6$ or $(3 \times 6) \times 4$ or $(4 \times 6) \times 3$
$32 \div n = 8$	$8 \times n = 32$
$n \times 6 = 36$	$36 \div 6 = n$
$54 \div 6 = n$	$6 \times n = 54$
73×4	Multiply 73×2, and then double the product
79×10	$790 \div 2 = 79 \times 5$
37×9	$(37 \times 10) - (37 \times 1)$

NAME:________________________________ DATE:______________

LESSON 2.3 RECORDING SHEET

Distributive Property

	=	
	=	
	=	
	=	
	=	
	=	

NAME:____ DATE:________________

LESSON 2.3 RECORDING SHEET

Commutative Property

	=	
	=	
	=	
	=	
	=	
	=	

NAME: ______________________ DATE: ______________

LESSON 2.3 RECORDING SHEET

Associative Property

	=	
	=	
	=	
	=	
	=	
	=	

NAME:__________ DATE:__________

LESSON 2.3 RECORDING SHEET

Inverse Operations

	=	
	=	
	=	
	=	
	=	
	=	

NAME: ______________________ DATE: ______________

LESSON 2.3 RECORDING SHEET

Strategies and Additional Problems

	=	
	=	
	=	
	=	
	=	
	=	

Operations and Algebraic Thinking

NAME:______________________________ DATE:______________

LESSON 2.3 PRACTICE

Multiplication and Division

1. Suppose your classmate does not know the product of 16 groups of 4. How might you help your friend calculate this answer by regrouping?

2. Read and study the following table. Then use the product of a number times 2 and the product of a number times 4 to help you create a rule for mentally solving a number times 8. Once you have discovered the rule, fill in the missing values (x, p, e, and n) in the table. What appears to be the relationship between a number times 4 and that same number times 8?

Number	Multiplied by 2	Multiplied by 4	Multiplied by 8
5	10	20	x
9	18	p	72
7	14	28	e
3	n	12	24

3. How does the rule you just described in the table above help you solve 67×8?

4. Apply the rule you just created to the following problems to check their accuracy.

   a. $4 \times 4 = (4 \times 2)n$

      n = ________

   b. $4 \times 6 = (2 \times 6)n$

      n = ________

5. How could Sedrick use the fact that $40 \times 8 = 320$ to help him determine the product of 47×8?

Operations and Algebraic Thinking

NAME:______________________________ DATE:______________

LESSON 2.3

Common Core Assessment Practice

Directions: Complete the problems below.

1. $56 = 8 \times N$
   a. $N = 9$
   b. $N = 7$
   c. $N = 8$
   d. $N = 6$

2. Maria has 3 boxes of candles. There are a total of 36 candles.
   a. If all of the candles are split equally among the boxes, how many candles are in each box? ________

   b. Which two expressions could be used to solve the previous problem?
      i. $3 = 36 \times C$
      ii. $36 = 3 \div C$
      iii. $36 = C \times 3$
      iv. $36 \div 3 = C$

   c. Explain your answer. How can both expressions be used to solve the problem?

3. 6 groups of n equals 42. n = ________
   a. 7
   b. 9
   c. 4
   d. 8

Operations and Algebraic Thinking

4. Skip count by 4 seven times. Demonstrate your skip counting on the number line provided. Skip counting by 4 seven times will result in what number? ________

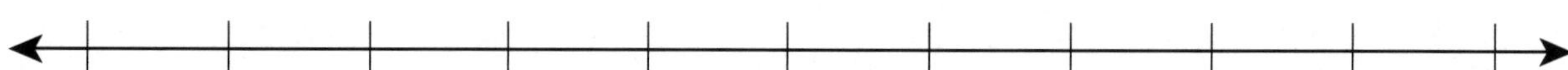

5. Select which division expression can be used to solve the following problem: $3 \times 12 = 36$.
   a. $12 \div 3$
   b. $36 \div 12$
   c. $3 \div 12$
   d. $12 \div 36$

LESSON 2.4

Problem Solving

Common Core State Standards

- 3.OA.3

Mathematical Practices

- 1, 4, and 7

Estimated Time

- 60 minutes

Teacher's Note. Students can either be given the four building sheets with measurements, or they can research the measurements of a building based on their interests to replicate. Some of the measurements included on the sheets have been rounded.

Key Terms

- Scaled model
- Height

Materials

- Lesson 2.4 Activity: Architect Arithmetic
- Lesson 2.4 Activity and Practice: Building Sheets
- Lesson 2.4 Common Core Assessment Practice
- Toothpicks
- Glue sticks
- Construction paper

Objectives

In this lesson, students will:

- utilize knowledge of multiplication and division to problem solve, and
- generate mathematical plans for solving various problem scenarios.

Lesson 2.4 Activity: Architect Arithmetic

In this activity, students will become architects and problem solve through constructing a building based on scaled measurements using toothpicks. They will work in pairs to answer questions about constructing replicas of famous structures around the world. Each pair of students will be given the four building sheets. They will choose the one building that interests them the most and answer the guiding questions on that page. Some information is provided on the building sheet and should be used to answer the questions. Once they have chosen their building and answered the guiding questions, they will understand that each toothpick represents a certain length. They will construct a scaled model of the building by gluing toothpicks to a piece of construction paper.

NAME:______________________________ DATE:________________

LESSON 2.4 ACTIVITY

Architect Arithmetic

Directions: Suppose you are no longer a student in this classroom, but instead an architect who is constructing a replica of a famous building. With a partner, choose one of the four famous buildings that you would like to construct, or one based on your own interests, and answer the questions on the corresponding building sheet. Use the information on the building sheet to help you build.

BUILDING OPTIONS

The Leaning Tower of Pisa **Location:** Pisa, Italy **Height:** 56 meters	**The Eiffel Tower** **Location:** Paris, France **Height:** Approximately 300 meters
The Statue of Liberty **Location:** New York, New York **Height:** Approximately 90 meters	**The Great Pyramid** **Location:** El Giza, Egypt **Height:** 450 feet
__________ **Location:** __________ **Height:** __________	__________ **Location:** __________ **Height:** __________

You will be given a set of toothpicks to use. Each toothpick stands for a certain length, so be sure to use the information carefully. Construct your building by gluing the toothpicks to your construction paper. The building will be a scaled model, which means it won't be the real height, but it will be an accurate model. The width of the building is your choice.

Extend Your Thinking

1. For each of the four buildings, determine a different amount that each toothpick could represent. There should be no remainders, and no toothpicks should be cut.

NAME:____ DATE:________________

LESSON 2.4 ACTIVITY & PRACTICE

Building Sheet

THE LEANING TOWER OF PISA

Location: Pisa, Italy

Height: 56 meters tall

You are the architect in charge of building a replica of the Leaning Tower of Pisa. Use the information and questions below to help plan your building.

1. The toothpicks each stand for 7 meters.
   a. How many toothpicks will you need to construct one side of the building that would represent the height of 56 meters? _______ Write an equation using a variable to represent the unknown. Solve.

   b. Prove your answer is reasonable.

Use the toothpicks that represent 7 meters each to build the Leaning Tower of Pisa. Remember to make sure the height represents 56 meters. After building the replica, answer the following questions.

2. If you were building the actual Leaning Tower of Pisa rather than a scaled model, it would have taken you a lot longer. Research how long it took to build the actual Leaning Tower of Pisa. If you were to break up the building process into 3 different time frames, how long would each time frame be?

3. You have been hired to paint a wall in the Leaning Tower of Pisa. The wall stands 56 meters tall and is 3 meters wide. To determine the amount of area on the plane figure that you must paint, you must multiply 56 meters by 3 meters. What is the product? _______

4. You decide to paint it in 28 days. How many square meters of the wall would you need to paint each day? ________

5. You only get paid every 14 square meters of painting. How many paychecks will you receive after completing the entire painting job? ________

6. If each paycheck equals $2,751.29, what is the grand total you will make for your replica? ________

7. If you needed $40,000.00 to start the next project, how much more money do you need to earn? ________

NAME:____ DATE:________________

LESSON 2.4 ACTIVITY & PRACTICE

Building Sheet

THE EIFFEL TOWER

Location: Paris, France

Height: Approximately 300 meters tall

You are the architect in charge of building a replica of the Eiffel Tower. Use the information and questions below to help plan your building.

1. The toothpicks each stand for 20 meters.
   - **a.** How many toothpicks will you need to construct one side of the building that would represent the height of 300 meters? _______ Write an equation using a variable to represent the unknown. Solve.
   - **b.** Prove your answer is reasonable.

Use the toothpicks that represent 20 meters each to build the Eiffel Tower. Remember to make sure the height represents 300 meters. After building the replica, answer the following questions.

2. For every 10 meters completed, you receive an extra day of vacation time.
   - **a.** How many extra days of vacation time can you earn on this project? _______ Write an equation using a variable to represent the unknown. Solve.
   - **b.** Use the inverse operation to check your work.

3. Eiffel Tower has 1,665 steps from the East Pillar to the top. You have been asked to replace all of them. Because this is such a tiring job, you are trying to schedule yourself breaks every so often.
   a. If you wanted to take a break after an equal number of steps, what options do you have? List as many as you can think of. (Hint: Think about divisibility rules. For example, I know I could rest after each set of 5 steps because 5 goes evenly into 1,665.)

   b. Choose one of your answers from Part A. How many breaks would you take? ________

4. You have been asked to consider building more steps. If you needed a total of 2,000 steps, how many more steps would you have to build? ________ Use addition to prove your answer is reasonable.

NAME: ______________________________ DATE: ______________

LESSON 2.4 ACTIVITY & PRACTICE

Building Sheet

THE STATUE OF LIBERTY

Location: New York, New York

Height: Approximately 90 meters tall

You are the architect in charge of building a replica of the Statue of Liberty. Use the information and questions below to help plan your building.

1. The toothpicks each stand for 5 meters.
   a. How many toothpicks will you need to construct one side of the building that would represent the height of 90 meters? _______ Write an equation using a variable to represent the unknown. Solve.

   b. Prove your answer is reasonable.

Use the toothpicks that represent 5 meters each to build the Statue of Liberty. Remember to make sure the height represents 90 meters. After building the replica, answer the following questions.

2. You have decided to build the replica in two different sections. Each part is equivalent in height.
   a. What is the height of each section? _______ Write an equation using a variable to represent the unknown. Solve.

   b. Use the inverse operation to check your work.

3. You decide to cover the front face of the tablet with copper. The front of the tablet is about 24 feet tall and about 14 feet wide. To decide how many square feet of copper you need to fill the plane surface, you must multiply 24 feet by 14 feet.
   a. What is the product? ________

   b. Write a division equation to check your work.

4. You were given two paychecks worth $1,274 each for building the Statue of Liberty replica. You were also given one paycheck worth $984.99 for painting the Statue of Liberty replica.
   a. How much total money did you make for building and painting the Statue of Liberty?

   b. How much more money did you get paid for building the statue than for painting the statue?

NAME:____ DATE:____________

LESSON 2.4 ACTIVITY & PRACTICE

Building Sheet

THE GREAT PYRAMID

Location: El Giza, Egypt
Height: 450 feet tall

You are the architect in charge of building a replica of the Great Pyramid. Use the information and questions below to help plan your building.

1. The toothpicks each stand for 45 feet.
   - **a.** How many toothpicks will you need to construct one side of the building that would represent the height of 450 feet? ________ Write an equation using a variable to represent the unknown. Solve.
   - **b.** Prove your answer is reasonable.

Use the toothpicks that represent 45 feet each to build the Great Pyramid. Remember to make sure the height represents 450 feet. After building the replica, answer the following questions.

2. You have decided to build the replica in five different but equal sections. Each part is equivalent in height.
   - **a.** What is the height of each section? ________ Write an equation using a variable to represent the unknown. Solve.
   - **b.** Use the inverse operation to check your work.

3. The base of the pyramid is 755 feet long.
   a. How much wider is the base of the pyramid than the height of the pyramid? ________

   b. Prove your answer is reasonable.

4. Leading into the Great Pyramid, there is an entranceway that leads to an underground chamber that is about 190 feet deep.
   a. If you were in charge of building doorways every 5 feet, and were paid $75 for each door, how much money would you make? ________

   b. If you had 3 employees helping you build the doorways, and each employee was paid $150.00, how much money would you have left? ________

NAME:______________________________ DATE:______________

LESSON 2.4

Common Core Assessment Practice

Directions: Complete the problems below.

1. Rebekah has 42 gloves in her closet. How many pair of gloves does she have?
   a. 22
   b. 12
   c. 21
   d. 84

2. Janiya brought donuts to give to her teachers for breakfast one morning. She brought 2-dozen donuts. Janiya gave each teacher 6 donuts. How many teachers did Janiya give donuts to?
   a. 6
   b. 5
   c. 4
   d. 12

3. Jonas has 84 baseball cards. He splits the cards evenly between 14 friends. How many cards does each friend receive?
   a. 7
   b. 6
   c. 3
   d. 5

4. The library has placed 74 books equally on 2 shelves. How many books are on each shelf? Write the multiplication equation using the variable b to represent the unknown.

5. When trying to determine the answer to Question 4, a student raised her hand and said that multiplication isn't the mathematical operation that should be used, so the problem can't be solved. Instead, she thought division should be used. How would you respond to this student if you were the teacher?

LESSON 2.5

Multistep Word Problems

Common Core State Standards

- 3.OA.8

Mathematical Practices

- 1, 2, 4, and 5

Estimated Time

- 60 minutes

Key Terms

- Variable
- Operations

Materials

- Lesson 2.5 Activity: Chef's Choice
- Lesson 2.5 Meal Request Cards
- Lesson 2.5 Food Fact Sheet
- Lesson 2.5 Menu
- Lesson 2.5 Practice: Multistep Word Problems
- Lesson 2.5 Common Core Assessment Practice

Objectives

In this lesson, students will:

- solve multistep word problems to solve real-world scenarios, and
- construct meal plans to solve word problems.

Lesson 2.5 Activity: Chef's Choice

In this activity, students will become chefs who are making meals for individuals with specific dietary needs. Each pair of students needs a set of meal request cards, which indicate the specific caloric requirements and requested food categories for the individuals. Each student will use the Food Fact Sheet to determine how many calories are in each food type. They will create a meal based on the information provided on the Meal Request Cards and Food Fact Sheets by filling in the menu. Each group of students will need four menus.

NAME:______________________________ DATE:______________

LESSON 2.5 ACTIVITY

Chef's Choice

Directions: Your expertise in math is needed to help people! You have now become a well-known chef in a large city at a popular restaurant. With a partner, you will create a menu for people based on their dietary needs. Choose one Meal Request Card at a time and read the request. Use the Food Fact Sheet to create a meal based on the needs and requests located on the card. Once you have discussed and chosen items, fill in the menu. Repeat these steps until all meal request cards have been completed.

Extend Your Thinking

The following are ideas for extending the activity:

1. Look at each menu you created and the corresponding meal request card. Are the options you chose the only options? If not, list the options for each category that each person could have received and still followed their calorie limit.

2. Research the daily caloric intake of boys and girls ages 9–14 and then create a corresponding meal based on the data obtained.

NAME:__________ DATE:__________

LESSON 2.5

Meal Request Cards

<table>
<tr>
<td>

1. I am only allowed 1,090 calories per meal. I cannot go over that amount and will be hungry if I eat less than 1,085 calories a meal.

My request is:
1 meat
1 vegetable
1 sweet

If I am cooking for two others and myself, what is the total amount of calories for each category?
Meat:
Vegetable:
Sweet:

</td>
<td>

2. I am only allowed 1,560 calories for my supper. I cannot go over that number and will be hungry if I eat much less than 1,560 calories at supper.

My request is at least:
2 meats
1 fruit
1 vegetable
2 carbohydrates
1 sweet

If I am cooking for four others and myself, what is the total amount of calories for each category?
Meat:
Fruit:
Vegetable:
Carbohydrates:
Sweet:

</td>
</tr>
<tr>
<td>

3. I am only allowed between 770–780 calories for lunch.

My request is:
2 servings of chicken
1 fruit
1 vegetable

If I am cooking one serving of chicken for each of the 7 members of my family plus the 2 servings that I will eat, how many total calories of chicken are being cooked?

</td>
<td>

4. I decide to eat 609 calories at lunch. My main meal must be spaghetti.

My request is:
1 serving of spaghetti
1 carbohydrate
1 sweet

If I decide to add a vegetable to my lunch but want to eat no more than 641 calories, what will I eat?

</td>
</tr>
</table>

NAME:______________________________ DATE:______________

LESSON 2.5

Food Fact Sheet

The provided calorie amounts are based on one serving and were obtained from http://caloriecount.com.

Meats

Steak: 847 cal.
Chicken: 306 cal.
Spaghetti: 221 cal.
Ham: 736 cal.
Turkey: 45 cal.

Vegetables

Broccoli: 50 cal.
Sweet potato: 114 cal.
Zucchini: 33 cal.
Tomato: 32 cal.
Cauliflower: 146 cal.

Sweets

Chocolate pie: 301 cal.
Pecan pie: 117 cal.

Fruits

Cantaloupe: 60 cal.
Strawberries: 47 cal.
Apple: 95 cal.

Carbohydrates

Roll: 87 cal.
Rice: 216 cal.
Baked potato: 129 cal.

NAME:______________________________ DATE:______________

LESSON 2.5

Menu

Meats:

Fruits:

Vegetables:

Carbohydrates:

Sweets:

NAME:____ DATE:_______________

LESSON 2.5 PRACTICE

Multistep Word Problems

Directions: Complete the problems below.

1. A small package of Sun Chips has 140 calories. The bag Timothy enjoyed contained 20 chips.
   a. If Timothy gave Kevin 4 chips, how many calories did Kevin consume? ________

   b. How many calories did Timothy consume? ________

   c. How many more calories did Timothy consume than Kevin? ________

2. The small bag of Cheetos contains 150 calories. There are 25 chips in the bag.
   a. How many calories does each chip have? ________

   b. How many chips should you give away if you are on a diet that requires only a 75-calorie snack? ________ Use the variable c to represent the unknown number of chips given away. Explain how you know your answer is reasonable.

3. One bag of Fritos has 160 calories. There are 20 chips in a bag.
   a. If you wanted to share the calories evenly among some friends, how many friends could receive an equal amount of calories? ________ Think of as many options as you can and prove your answer is reasonable.

   b. If Dexter only wanted to consume 120 calories, how many chips should he discard? ________

Extend Your Thinking

1. Choose a snack item and look at the nutrition label. Create questions about the food product that will make your classmates add, subtract, multiply, or divide to solve.

2. Look up the dietary guidelines for caloric intakes per day for adults. Then design meals using caloriecount.com that reflect the caloric intake guidelines for adults. Finally, create a menu that displays your meal options.

NAME:______________________________ DATE:______________

LESSON 2.5

Common Core Assessment Practice

Directions: Complete the problems below.

1. For the swimming party, Julia's mom is filling old baby pools with water. Every time she fills 8 pools, she discovers leaks in half of the pools. How many pools does Julia's mom need to fill if she must have 72 baby pools full of water?

2. Fifty-four people came to the Dinosaur Science night. Each of the 54 students created 3 fossil molds. If 14 of the fossil molds broke, how many fossil molds were not broken?

3. Penelope made 75 brownies for teacher appreciation week at her school. She brought 16 on Monday, 23 on Tuesday, and the rest on Wednesday. How many brownies did Penelope bring to school on Wednesday?

4. During class economy day, Alicia purchased 4 basketballs for $14 each. She paid for the basketballs with three $20 bills. How much change did Alicia receive?

5. Susie, Beth, and Carlos decided to combine their money to buy a gift for their parents. Susie has $23, Beth has three times as much as Susie, and Carlos has $9 less than Beth. How much money does Carlos have?

LESSON 2.6

Patterns

Common Core State Standards

- 3.OA.9

Mathematical Practices

- 1, 2, 3, 6, and 7

Estimated Time

- 60 minutes

Key Terms

- Sequence
- Input/output

Materials

- Lesson 2.6 Activity: What's the Pattern?
- Lesson 2.6 What's the Pattern? Chart 1
- Lesson 2.6 What's the Pattern? Number Cards 1
- Lesson 2.6 What's the Pattern? Chart 2
- Lesson 2.6 What's the Pattern? Number Cards 2
- Lesson 2.6 What's the Pattern? Chart 3
- Lesson 2.6 What's the Pattern? Number Cards 3
- Lesson 2.6 Practice: Patterns
- Lesson 2.6 Completed Multiplication Chart
- Lesson 2.6 Blank Multiplication Chart
- Lesson 2.6 Common Core Assessment Practice
- Bag for cards
- Glue sticks
- Colors

Objectives

In this lesson, students will:

- analyze number sequences to determine patterns, and
- discover patterns within numbers.

Lesson 2.6 Activity: What's the Pattern?

In this activity, students will be given What's the Pattern? Number Cards for each What's the Pattern? Chart. Students will read the rule for the chart and then place the numbers in the correct spot on the input/output chart. Once the numbers are paired correctly, they need to be placed in order from least to greatest and glued down. Students will then answer the questions on the page before going to the next chart. The next chart needs to be copied on a different color paper along with the number cards. The charts and corresponding numbers need to be copied on colored paper, cut out, and placed in separate bags before students begin this activity.

Teacher's Note. If colored paper is not available, hand out one set of cards and one chart at a time. As students finish each chart, they can turn in their work and pick up the next chart and number cards.

NAME:______________________________ DATE:______________

LESSON 2.6 ACTIVITY
What's the Pattern?

Directions: Input/output charts are just like puzzles. Your powerful puzzle skills are needed to place numbers in the correct places depending on given clues. Work with a partner and choose a What's the Pattern? Chart and gather the bag of corresponding number cards.

Use the clues given to solve the puzzle by filling in the blanks with the numbers. Place all of the numbers so you and your partner can see them. Once you have made all of the input/output matches, place them in order from least to greatest. Glue the numbers to the chart, and then answer the questions.

Extend Your Thinking

1. You should have discovered patterns that occur when multiplying and adding by certain numbers. See if you can find any patterns dealing with division. What happens when you divide an even number by an even number? What about when you divide an even number by an odd number? An odd number by an even number?

2. Create your own input/output chart with numbers in the correct place and have a partner determine the rule.

Input	Output

NAME:____________________ DATE:__________

LESSON 2.6

What's the Pattern? Chart 1

The rule for the chart is to add 7.

Input	Output

1. Once you have filled in the chart, look for a pattern for adding even and odd numbers. What do you notice about the sum of an even number plus an odd number?

2. Generate a few more number sentences to check to see that your hypothesis is correct.

NAME: ______________________ DATE: ______________

LESSON 2.6

What's the Pattern? Number Cards 1

2	9
4	11
6	13
8	15
10	17

NAME:______________________________ DATE:______________

LESSON 2.6

What's the Pattern? Chart 2

The rule for the chart is to multiply by 3.

Input	Output

1. Use the information in the chart to help you answer the following questions.
   a. What do you notice about multiplying an odd number times an even number?

   b. What do you notice about multiplying an odd number times an odd number?

2. Generate some number sentences of your own to check your hypothesis.

NAME:________________________________ DATE:____________

LESSON 2.6

What's the Pattern? Number Cards 2

7	21
10	30
13	39
16	48
19	57
22	66

NAME:______________________________ DATE:______________

LESSON 2.6

What's the Pattern? Chart 3

The rule for the chart is to multiply by 4.

Input	Output

1. Look for a pattern in the output side of the table.
   a. What do you notice?

   b. What do you notice about multiplying an odd number times an even number?

2. Bradley doesn't know what 34 × 4 equals. Tony told him to calculate 34 × 2 and then double the product. Do you agree with Tony? Why or why not? Provide an example to support your answer.

NAME:______________________________ DATE:______________

LESSON 2.6

What's the Pattern? Number Cards 3

1	4
2	8
3	12
4	16
5	20
6	24

LESSON 2.6 PRACTICE

Patterns

Directions: Complete the problems below.

1. On the completed multiplication chart provided, highlight one row and one column that show the order in which factors are multiplied doesn't change the product.

2. On the blank multiplication sheet provided, use the following colors to solve certain facts.
   a. Solve all of the even numbers times even numbers in blue. What do you notice about the products?

   b. Solve all of the even numbers times odd numbers in red. What do you notice about the products?

   c. Solve all of the odd numbers times odd numbers in green. What do you notice about the products?

3. Now think about addition. Do you think the patterns of odd and even number products will be the same for the sum of numbers? Support your answer with evidence.

Extend Your Thinking

1. Analyze the multiplication chart to discover more patterns created. Highlight your patterns in a different color.

NAME:_______________ DATE:_______________

LESSON 2.6

Completed Multiplication Chart

X	0	1	2	3	4	5	6	7	8	9	10	11	12
0	0	0	0	0	0	0	0	0	0	0	0	0	0
1	0	1	2	3	4	5	6	7	8	9	10	11	12
2	0	2	4	6	8	10	12	14	16	18	20	22	24
3	0	3	6	9	12	15	18	21	24	27	30	33	36
4	0	4	8	12	16	20	24	28	32	36	40	44	48
5	0	5	10	15	20	25	30	35	40	45	50	55	60
6	0	6	12	18	24	30	36	42	48	54	60	66	72
7	0	7	14	21	28	35	42	49	56	63	70	77	84
8	0	8	16	24	32	40	48	56	64	72	80	88	96
9	0	9	18	27	36	45	54	63	72	81	90	99	108
10	0	10	20	30	40	50	60	70	80	90	100	110	120
11	0	11	22	33	44	55	66	77	88	99	110	121	132
12	0	12	24	36	48	60	72	84	96	108	120	132	144

NAME:____ DATE:________________

LESSON 2.6

Blank Multiplication Chart

X	0	1	2	3	4	5	6	7	8	9	10	11	12
0													
1													
2													
3													
4													
5													
6													
7													
8													
9													
10													
11													
12													

NAME:____________________________ DATE:____________

LESSON 2.6

Common Core Assessment Practice

Directions: Complete the problems below.

1. Write a four-number pattern, starting at any number you choose, that follows this rule: Multiply by 7.

2. What is the rule to the following pattern?

   1,654; 1,634; 1,614; 1,594

   a. Multiply by 2
   b. Divide by 2
   c. Add 12
   d. Subtract 20

3. The following pattern was created by multiplying each number by n. What does n equal?

   15, 45, 135, 405

   a. $n = 3$
   b. $n = 5$
   c. $n = 7$
   d. $n = 2$

4. Selma mowed lawns for extra money. The table shows the amount of yards mowed and the amount of money earned. If Selma continues to be paid in the same way, fill in the rest of the chart.

Lawns Mowed	Money
1	$19.00
2	$26.00
3	
4	
5	$47.00
6	

Operations and Algebraic Thinking

SECTION III

Number and Operations—Fractions

LESSON 3.1

Fractions and Number Lines

Common Core State Standards

- 3.NF.1
- 3.NF.2

Mathematical Practices

- 1, 4, and 7

Estimated Time

- 60 minutes

Key Terms

- Partition

Materials

- Lesson 3.1 Activity: Fractional Lengths
- Lesson 3.1 Practice: Fractions and Number Lines
- Lesson 3.1 Common Core Assessment Practice
- Straws
- Dry erase markers
- Scissors
- Rulers

Objectives

In this lesson, students will:

- partition wholes into fractional pieces, and
- represent fractions on a number line.

Lesson 3.1 Activity: Fractional Lengths

In this activity, students are in charge of the plumbing at a new construction site. Students will measure and cut various lengths of pipe (straws) based on fractional measurements. Each pair of students needs eight straws that are about 8 inches long. The first straw represents the whole, and is never cut. All fractional measurements are referencing this whole. Students will read a scenario and then cut various straws into $\frac{1}{2}$, $\frac{1}{4}$, $\frac{1}{8}$, $\frac{1}{6}$, $\frac{1}{8}$, $\frac{1}{10}$, and $\frac{1}{12}$. You can give students these measurements, or have them use a ruler to determine how long each fractional piece should be. After reading each scenario and after each pipe is cut, students will locate and mark that fraction on an 8-inch number line (p. 96). Students can use the fractional pieces they cut to help them locate where the fraction should be located on the number line.

NAME:____ DATE:________________

LESSON 3.1 ACTIVITY

Fractional Lengths

Directions: Because of your excellent calculation skills, you have been hired to complete a tricky measurement job dealing with the plumbing system at a new construction site. You will work with a partner to measure various straws that represent the pipes to fit the needs of the construction site. One straw (pipe) represents one whole and every fraction that you and your partner work with today will be related to this whole. Make sure to reference this whole when needed, and also make sure that this pipe never gets cut, or you could have a major leak and lose your job! Complete the steps below, using the number line on page 96.

1. In the kitchen, under the sink, the contractor has asked you to make two $\frac{1}{2}$ pieces of pipe.
   a. How many total sections will you have after you mark the pipe with your dry erase marker? ________
   b. If the whole pipe is 8 inches long, how long will each piece be? ________
   c. Now follow the directions to cut the pipe and label the number line.
2. The contractor has asked for some pipes that are $\frac{1}{4}$ of the whole pipe.
   a. How many total sections will you have after you mark the pipe with your dry erase marker? ________
   b. If the whole pipe is about 8 inches long, how long will each piece be? ________
   c. Now follow the directions to cut the pipe and label the number line.
3. To fix an issue in the bathroom sink, you are asked to cut pipe. You need each piece to represent $\frac{1}{5}$ of the whole pipe.
   a. How many total sections will you have after you mark the pipe with your dry erase marker? ________
   b. If the whole pipe is about 8 inches long, how long will each piece be? ________
   c. Now follow the directions to cut the pipe and label the number line.

4. Another issue with the plumbing has caused you to have to cut even smaller pieces of pipe. You now need pipe that is $\frac{1}{6}$ the size of the original pipe.
   a. How many total sections will you have after you mark the pipe with your dry erase marker? ________
   b. If the whole pipe is about 8 inches long, how long will each piece be? ________
   c. Now follow the directions to cut the pipe and label the number line.
5. To fix an outside pipe, the contractor has asked you to created a piece of pipe that is $\frac{1}{8}$ the size of the whole pipe.
   a. How many total sections will you have after you mark the pipe with your dry erase marker? ________
   b. If the whole pipe is about 8 inches long, how long will each piece be? ________
   c. Now follow the directions to cut the pipe and label the number line.
6. You realize that $\frac{1}{8}$ is not the size pipe you needed to fix the outside plumbing problem, so you cut pipe the size of $\frac{1}{10}$ of the whole.
   a. How many total sections will you have after you mark the pipe with your dry erase marker? ________
   b. If the whole pipe is about 8 inches long, how long will each piece be? ________
   c. Now follow the directions to cut the pipe and label the number line.
7. Finally, the last job requires a piece of pipe that is $\frac{1}{12}$ the length of the whole pipe.
   a. How many total sections will you have after you mark the pipe with your dry erase marker? ________
   b. If the whole pipe is about 8 inches long, how long will each piece be? ________
   c. Now follow the directions to cut the pipe and label the number line.

Extend Your Thinking

1. Suppose the job requires the use of a pipe $2\frac{1}{3}$ inches in length. How could you represent this measurement with the straws?

NAME: ______________________________ DATE: ______________

LESSON 3.1 PRACTICE

Fractions and Number Lines

1. The local movie theater is tracking attendance at the shows.
   a. On Thursday, there were originally 18 people at the movie, but 3 people left. What fraction of people left? ________

   b. What fraction of people remained? ________

2. On Friday night, 18 people entered the theater, but 6 people left early.
   a. What fraction of people left? ________

   b. What fraction of people remained? ________

3. Did the movie have better attendance on Thursday night or Friday night? Explain your answer.

4. The movie theater sold pizzas for people to snack on while watching the movie.
   a. The first pizza displayed was pepperoni and was cut into 8 slices. Four pieces were eaten. Draw a number line below, and label the fraction of pieces that were sold.

   b. The next pizza displayed was sausage and was also cut into eighths, but only 2 slices were eaten. On the same number line, label the fraction of pieces that were sold.
   c. Look at the number line and the two fractions. Which pizza sold more pieces? ________

5. Some people bought whole pizzas to eat during the movie. The chicken pizzas were sold in small sizes and large sizes. Jeremiah purchased the small pizza and ate the whole thing. Kerri purchased the large pizza, and she also ate the whole thing. Kerri says she ate the same amount as Jeremiah, but Jeremiah says he ate less. Who do you agree with? Explain your answer.

Extend Your Thinking

1. Determine what fraction of your classmates has brown eyes. What fraction has blue eyes? Collect the data. Then represent the data on a number line.

NAME:____________________ DATE:__________

LESSON 3.1

Common Core Assessment Practice

Directions: Complete the problems below.

1. Shade $\frac{3}{4}$ of the rectangle.

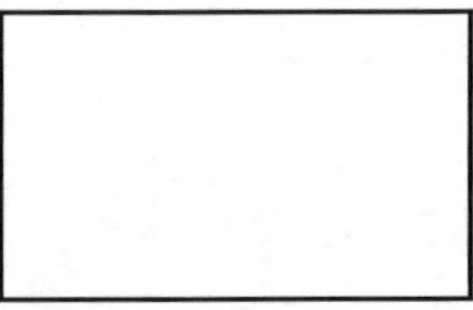

2. Shade $\frac{1}{3}$ of the whole circle.

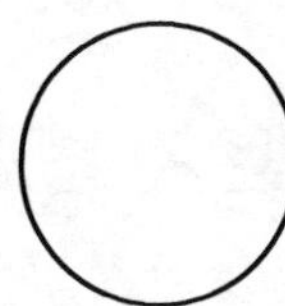

3. Which number is not represented by the picture?

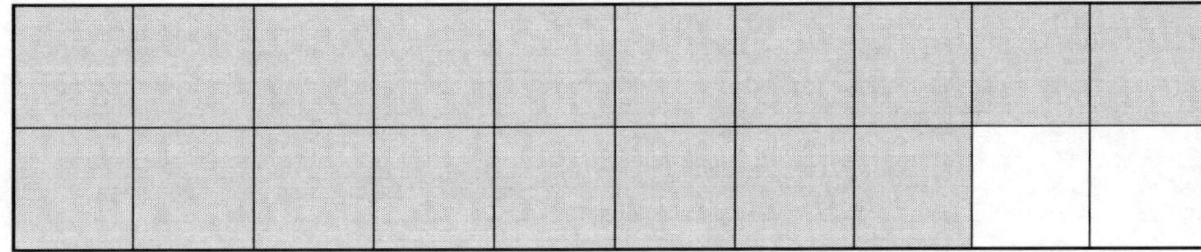

   a. 1.8

   b. $1\frac{8}{10}$

   c. $\frac{18}{10}$

   d. 8

Number and Operations—Fractions

4. Place a dot on the number line where $\frac{5}{12}$ would be located. Explain why you placed the dot in that spot.

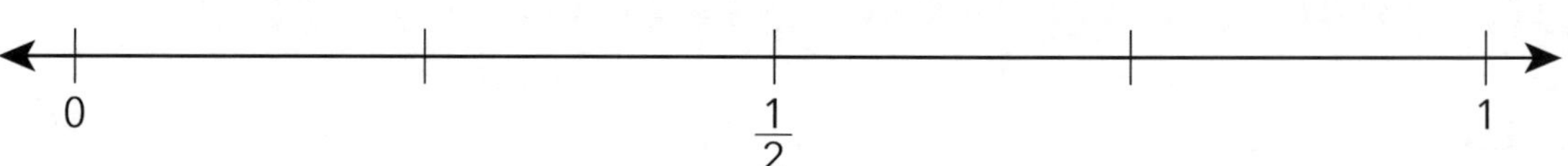

5. Place a dot on the number line where $\frac{7}{8}$ would be located. Explain why you placed a dot in that spot.

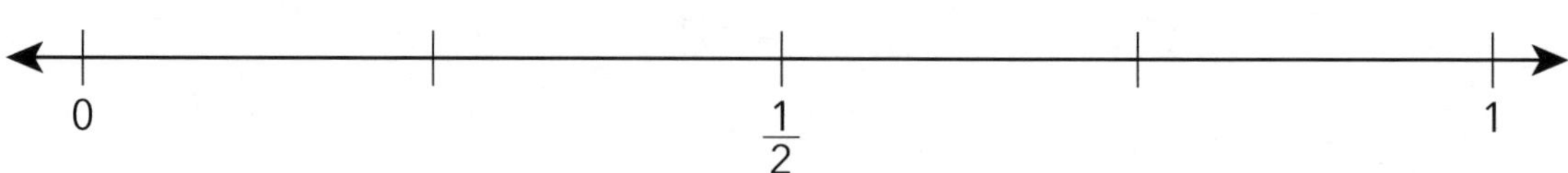

LESSON 3.2

Equivalent Fractions

Common Core State Standards

- 3.NF.3a
- 3.NF.3b
- 3.NF.3c

Mathematical Practices

- 1, 2, 3, 4, 6, 7, and 8

Estimated Time

- 60 minutes

Key Terms

- Equivalent

Materials

- Lesson 3.2 Activity: Equivalence
- Lesson 3.2 Fraction Cards
- Lesson 3.2 Practice: Equivalent Fractions
- Lesson 3.2 Common Core Assessment Practice

Objectives

In this lesson, students will:

- create equivalent fractions, and
- represent a whole in various ways.

Lesson 3.2 Activity: Equivalence

In this activity, students will be given a bag of fraction cards. The cards each have a representation of a fraction on them. Some cards have pictures, and others have number lines. The students will be given a fraction on their activity sheet and will find two cards that are equivalent to the given fraction. The students will then create another equivalent fraction using the guided questions provided on the activity sheet. Students will support their matches with an explanation.

NAME:______________________________________ DATE:_______________

LESSON 3.2 ACTIVITY

Equivalence

Directions: Fractions can be written in numerous ways, depending how each individual thinks about them. Put on your thinking cap, and try to determine several ways to write fractions by working with a partner to find two fraction cards that are equivalent to each of the fractions on the activity sheet.

Once you have found a pair of fractions equivalent to the fraction on the activity sheet, answer the question. That will help you create yet another equivalent fraction. Be sure to discuss with your partner and provide reasoning as to how you knew the fractions were equivalent.

Given Fraction	Equivalent Fraction Card	Equivalent Fraction Card	Create Equivalent Fraction
$\frac{2}{8}$			Divide a box into 24 equal sections. How many sections should be shaded to represent $\frac{2}{8}$?
$\frac{4}{6}$			If 20 boxes were being counted and shaded (numerator), how many total sections would the box have to be broken into (denominator)?

Given Fraction	Equivalent Fraction Card	Equivalent Fraction Card	Create Equivalent Fraction
$\frac{3}{10}$ 			If the same length number line was broken into 20 equal sections, where would the tick mark have to be to create an equivalent fraction?
○□□○○○□□○□ What fraction of the shapes are circles?			If the denominator of a fraction was 28, what would the numerator have to be to create an equivalent fraction?

Extend Your Thinking

1. Think of a fraction. Now create three fractions that are equivalent to your fraction. Represent each fraction with a picture or on the number line.

2. Think about the mixed number $5\frac{3}{4}$. Draw a picture to represent the number. Then locate and label the number on the given number line.

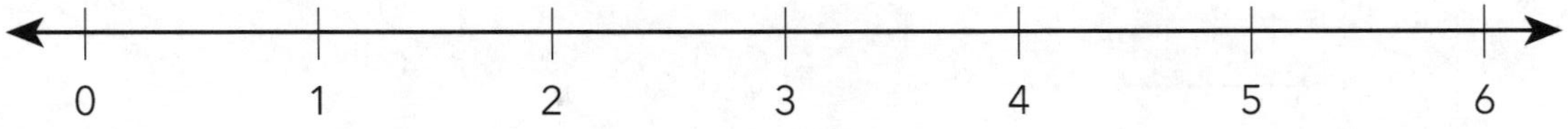

NAME:______________________________ DATE:______________

LESSON 3.2

Fraction Cards

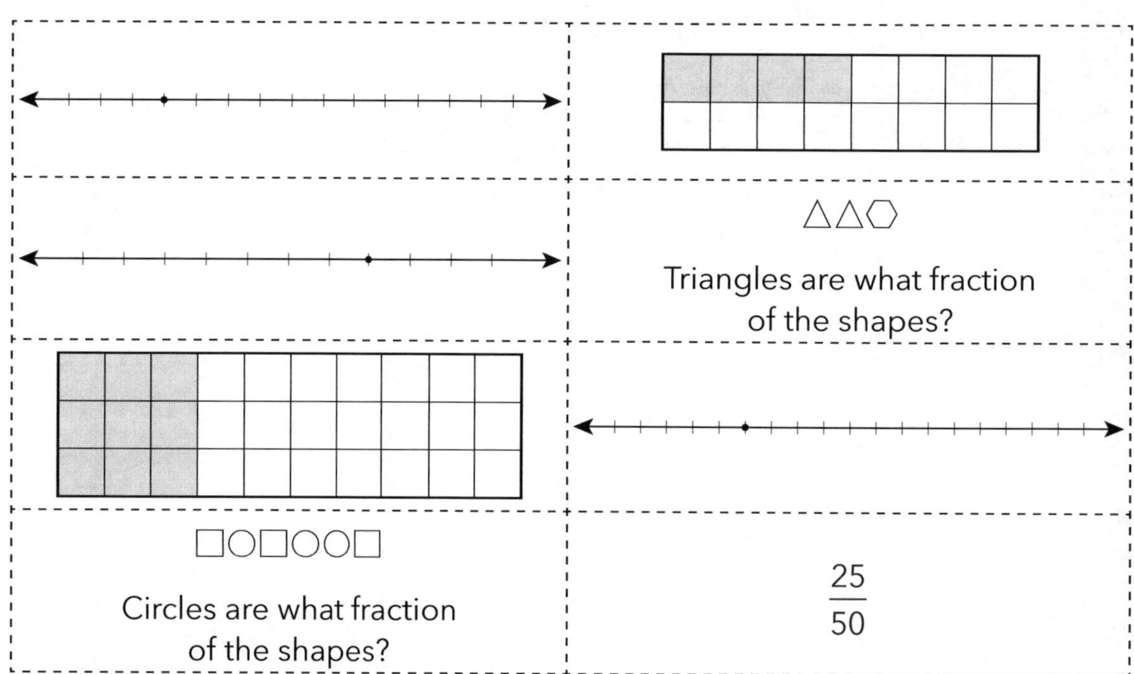

Number and Operations—Fractions

NAME:______________________________ DATE:______________

LESSON 3.2 PRACTICE

Equivalent Fractions

Directions: Complete the problems below.

1. Carlie and Ian were celebrating their birthdays. Suppose Carlie cut her cake into 9 pieces as shown below and Ian cut his cake into 5 pieces as shown below. Carlie says to Ian that her birthday cake was bigger, because she was able to cut her cake in to more pieces.
   a. If the pictures below are accurate, how should Ian respond?

Carlie

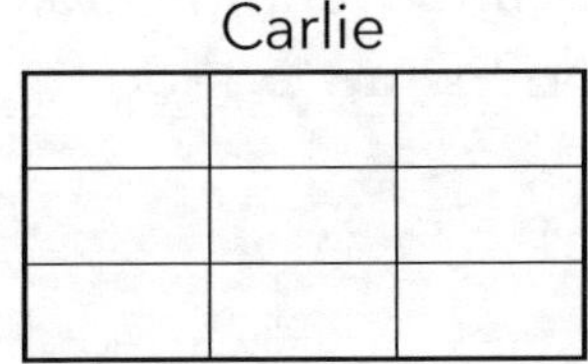

Ian

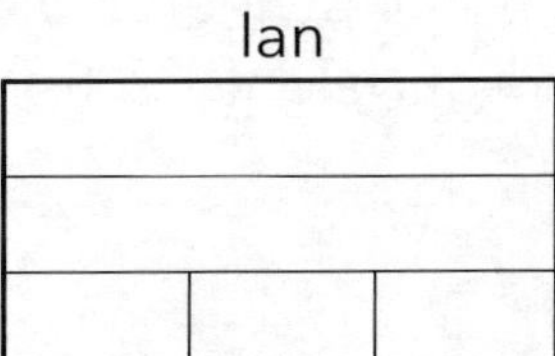

   b. How could you cut the cakes to make them look alike? Draw a model of your answer below.

2. Each pizza at the birthday party was sliced into 9 pieces. Ian ate all of the slices in one pizza.
   a. What fraction of the pizza did he eat? ________

   b. What is another way to represent the amount of pizza Ian consumed?

3. Carlie says that altogether, all of the guests ate 10 whole pizzas. How could you represent that as a fraction if you are actually referring to a number larger than one whole? Explain your fraction.

Extend Your Thinking

1. How does multiplying or dividing the numerator and denominator of a fraction create an equivalent fraction? What is happening? Draw a model to show your thinking.

NAME:________________________________ DATE:____________

LESSON 3.2

Common Core Assessment Practice

Directions: Complete the problems below.

1. You need to purchase $\frac{3}{4}$ of a yard of fabric from the fabric store. When you arrived, you did not see any fabric pieces labeled $\frac{3}{4}$ of a yard. Which of the following labels is equivalent to $\frac{3}{4}$ yard?

   a. $\frac{1}{2}$

   b. $\frac{6}{8}$

   c. $\frac{3}{9}$

   d. $\frac{1}{4}$

2. Explain how you know that the piece of fabric you chose is equivalent to $\frac{3}{4}$ yard.

3. You bought four pieces of fabric. The employee cuts the fabric into four equal parts from a larger piece of fabric (see the picture below). Write two different fractions that show the part of the bigger piece of fabric that you bought.

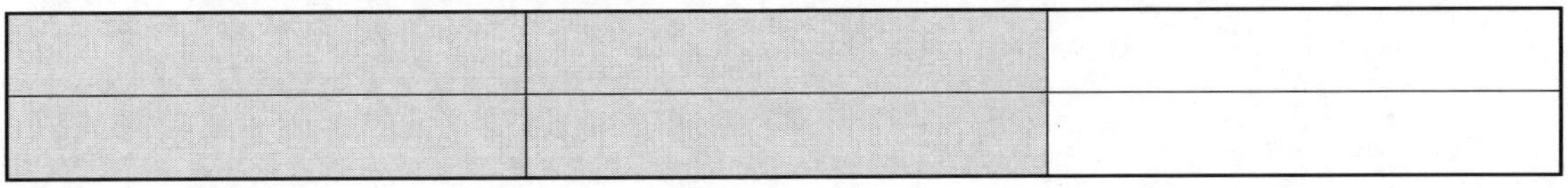

4. From the fabric store, you also needed to purchase $\frac{5}{8}$ yard of yarn. You locate yarn labeled $\frac{5}{8}$ inch. Is this the correct amount of yarn that you should purchase? Why or why not?

5. Draw a picture that shows how 42 divided by 2 is 21.

LESSON 3.3

Comparing Fractions

Common Core State Standards

- 3.NF.3d

Mathematical Practices

- 1, 2, 3, 6, and 8

Estimated Time

- 60 minutes

Key Terms

- Common denominator
- Numerator
- Probability

Materials

- Lesson 3.3 Activity: Comparing Fractions
- Lesson 3.3 Comparing Fractions Chart
- Lesson 3.3 Die A
- Lesson 3.3 Die B
- Lesson 3.3 Practice: Comparing Fractions
- Lesson 3.3 Common Core Assessment Practice

Objectives

In this lesson, students will:

- compare fractions with like denominators or numerators,
- justify fraction comparisons with visual models, and
- calculate the probability of a given event.

Lesson 3.3 Activity: Comparing Fractions

In this activity, students will compare fractions by rolling the dice provided. Die A will be used in the first round, and students will try to roll the largest fraction. Die B will be used in the second round, and students will try to roll the smallest fraction. In the first round, Partner A will roll Die A, and Partner B will decide the probability of rolling a larger fraction using the same die. Partner B will then roll the die, and the two students will discuss who rolled the larger fraction. Students will decide how many eighths larger one fraction is than the other. During play, students will complete the chart on the activity sheet and respond to the questions.

During the second round, the students should switch partner roles. Partner A (formerly Partner B) will roll Die B, and Partner B (formerly Partner A) will determine the probability of rolling a smaller fraction. Partner B will then roll the die, and the two students will discuss who rolled the smaller fraction and why. During play, students will complete the chart on the activity sheet and respond to the questions. Students will play three rounds for a total of six rolls.

NAME:________________________________ DATE:________________

LESSON 3.3 ACTIVITY

Comparing Fractions

Directions: Who can roll the largest or smallest fraction? Let's find out! You and a partner will work together to compare fractions by playing a dice game.

In the first round, Partner A will roll Die A, and Partner B will decide the probability of rolling a larger fraction using the same die. Partner B will then attempt to roll a larger fraction. Discuss with each other who rolled the larger fraction and by how many eighths. Record your work on the chart and answer the questions as you play. Continue until the two of you each roll three times.

For the second round, Partner B will roll first. This time, after Partner B rolls Die B, Partner A will determine the probability of rolling a smaller fraction. Partner A will then roll the die. Discuss with each other who rolled the smaller fraction and how you know. Record your work on the chart and answer the questions as you play. Continue until the two of you each roll three times.

Extend Your Thinking

1. Make your own dice with fractions of unlike numerators and denominators, and have your classmates compare them by using their knowledge of multiples.

NAME:______________________ DATE:__________

LESSON 3.3

Comparing Fractions Chart

1. Play the first round with Die A and fill in the chart as you play.

Partner A's Roll	Chances of Rolling a Larger Fraction	Partner B's Roll	Who Rolled the Larger Fraction?	How Many Eighths Larger?
1				
2				
3				
4				
5				
6				

2. Order all of your combined rolls from least to greatest. Draw a number line and represent each roll on the number line. Duplicate rolls do not need to be recorded more than once.

3. Play the second round with Die B and fill in the chart as you play.

Partner A's Roll	Chances of Rolling a Smaller Fraction	Partner B's Roll	Who Rolled the Smaller Fraction?	How Do You Know?
1				
2				
3				
4				
5				
6				

NAME:______________________ DATE:______________

LESSON 3.3

Die A

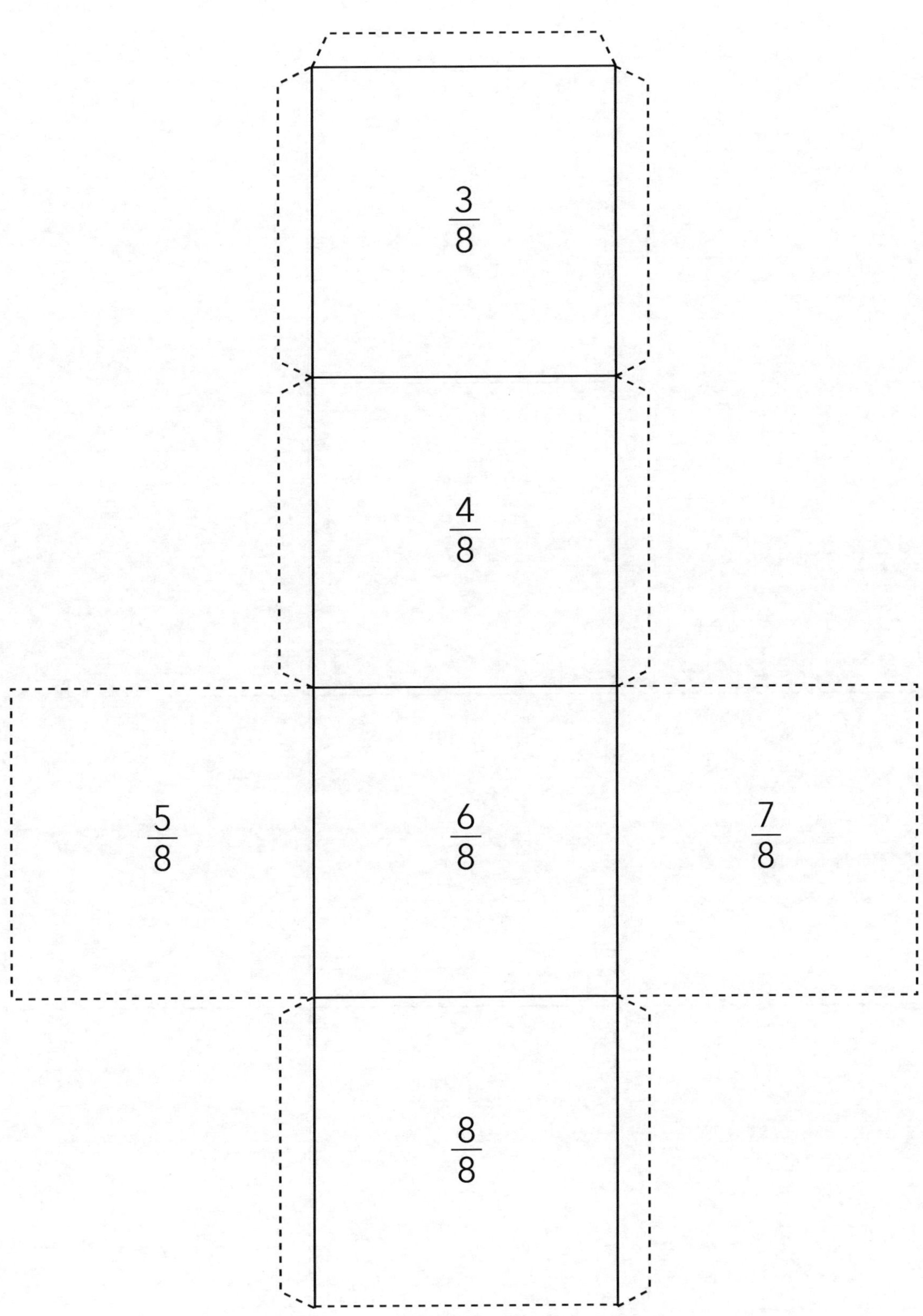

NAME:________________________________ DATE:______________

LESSON 3.3

Die B

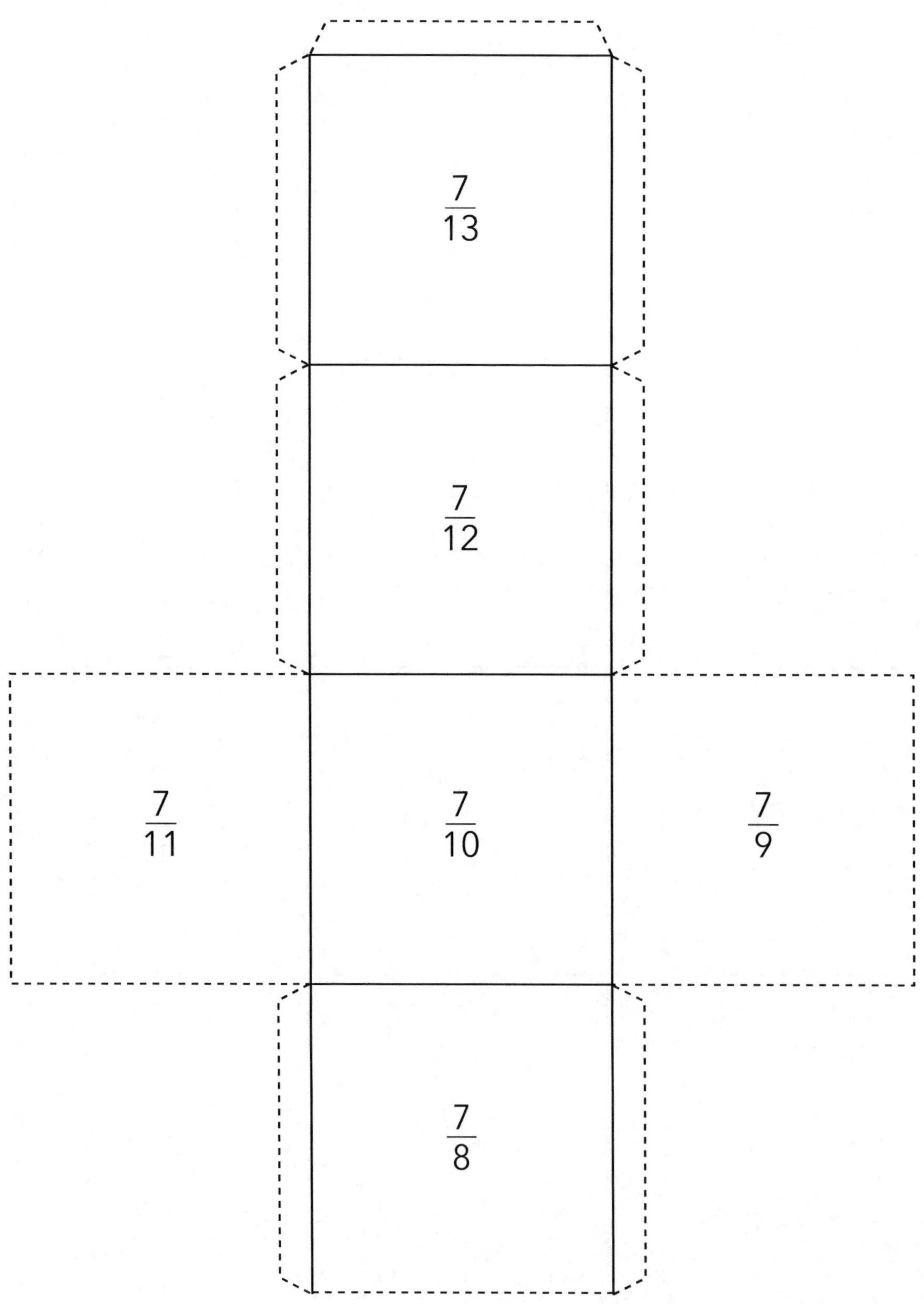

Number and Operations—Fractions

NAME:______________________________ DATE:______________

LESSON 3.3 PRACTICE

Comparing Fractions

Directions: Complete the problems below.

1. Marvin was disappointed because he only received $\frac{1}{5}$ of a pie and says that his friend Peter received more pie because his dessert was cut from the same size pie, but he got to eat $\frac{1}{7}$ of the pie. Who ate more pie? Explain using pictures and words.

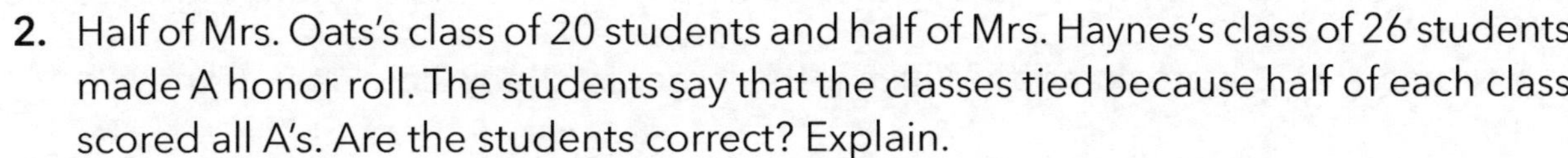

2. Half of Mrs. Oats's class of 20 students and half of Mrs. Haynes's class of 26 students made A honor roll. The students say that the classes tied because half of each class scored all A's. Are the students correct? Explain.

3. Make a generalization about comparing fractions with common denominators that are referring to the same whole.

4. Make a generalization about comparing fractions with numerators that are alike but do not have the same whole.

NAME:______________________________ DATE:______________

LESSON 3.3

Common Core Assessment Practice

Directions: Complete the problems below.

1. Which fraction is smaller than $\frac{7}{10}$?
   - a. $\frac{9}{10}$
   - b. $\frac{6}{10}$
   - c. $\frac{8}{10}$
   - d. $\frac{11}{10}$

2. The local movie shop is having a sale. Of the movies that Claudia buys, $\frac{4}{5}$ are drama and $\frac{4}{7}$ were comedy. Which is the larger fraction? How do you know?

3. Which sequence of fractions is ordered from least to greatest?
   - a. $\frac{2}{5}, \frac{1}{2}, \frac{1}{5}$
   - b. $\frac{7}{8}, \frac{7}{9}, \frac{9}{9}$
   - c. $\frac{4}{8}, \frac{4}{7}, \frac{4}{9}$
   - d. $\frac{2}{9}, \frac{2}{8}, \frac{2}{5}$

4. Which fraction is larger than $\frac{3}{5}$?

a. $\frac{3}{4}$

b. $\frac{3}{7}$

c. $\frac{3}{11}$

d. $\frac{3}{13}$

SECTION IV

Measurement and Data

LESSON 4.1

Time

Common Core State Standards

- 3.MD.1

Mathematical Practices

- 1, 4, 5, and 6

Estimated Time

- 60 minutes

Key Terms

- Schedule

Materials

- Lesson 4.1 Activity: Scheduling
- Lesson 4.1 School Schedule
- Lesson 4.1 Practice: Time
- Lesson 4.1 Common Core Assessment Practice

Objectives

In this lesson, students will:

- create a schedule based on given time requirements, and
- solve elapsed time problems related to real-world scenarios.

Lesson 4.1 Activity: Scheduling

In this lesson, students will create a school day schedule based on given requirements. They are asked to include math, science, social studies, reading, language, physical education, music, lunch, and recess. All classes except music are designated with a specific length of time (they will have to decide how long music class will be, given the other parameters). Students are aware that school starts at 8:05, and lasts for exactly 6 hours and 36 minutes. Students will arrange the subjects in any order they desire, as long as the day starts and ends on time. In addition, they are restricted by two 15-minute breaks that cannot be changed.

NAME:____ DATE:______________

LESSON 4.1 ACTIVITY

Scheduling

Directions: Complete the steps below.

It is your chance to plan your school schedule! Your principal has asked for you to help design the perfect daily schedule for third graders, but has given you some specific requirements. With your partner, read the following information carefully to help you make a schedule of a school day that meets all of the principal's requests.

Requirements

- The school day starts at 8:05 a.m.
- The school day lasts exactly 6 hours and 36 minutes.
- You have a 15-minute break that starts at 12:47.
- You have a second 15-minute break that starts at 1:32.
- Each class lasts for a specific amount of minutes, except music:
  - Recess: 15 min.
  - Lunch: 22 min.
  - Math: 90 min.
  - Science: 35 min.
  - Social Studies: 30 min.
  - Reading: 90 min.
  - Language: 27 min.
  - Physical Education: 30 min.
  - Music: _____ min.

You will need to determine the length of your music class based on the other provided information.

Extend Your Thinking

1. Create a Saturday schedule that you believe would be the perfect Saturday. Give yourself a number of specific requirements and a start and end time.

NAME:______________________________ DATE:______________

LESSON 4.1

School Schedule

Activity	Start Time	End Time	Number of Minutes
School Day Starts at 8:05			

Do not forget that your scheduled breaks are at a certain time and last exactly 15 minutes. You have a 15-minute break that starts at 12:47, and your second 15-minute break starts at 1:32.

Measurement and Data

NAME: ______________________________ DATE: ______________

LESSON 4.1 PRACTICE

Time

Directions: Complete the problems below.

1. You are a business owner, and Mark and Jody work for you. They have put in their request for Wednesday's schedule: Jody cannot work her usual hours on Wednesday, but has agreed to come open up the business for you. She can be there at 8:15 a.m., but must leave for an appointment no later than 9:00 a.m., so she requests that someone relieve her at 8:57 a.m. Mark can't come in to relieve Jody until 9:25 a.m., so you have to fill in during the time between Jody leaving and Mark arriving.
   a. How long did Jody work until you were able to take over the shift? ________

   b. How long did you work until Mark was able to take over the shift? ________

   c. If you close for lunch at 12:05 p.m., and Mark worked until then without taking a break, how long did he work? ________

   d. Jody only gets paid if she works a full hour. How many minutes short was she? ________

2. You leave work and drive for 25 minutes to the nearest café for lunch. After eating for 30 minutes, and driving 25 minutes back to work, it is now 12:45 p.m.
   a. What time did you leave work? ________

   b. Model your work on the number line below.

Measurement and Data

c. What time did you get to the café? ________

d. What time did you finish eating? ________

e. How long were you gone from work altogether? ________

3. Draw a clock similar to one that would hang on a wall. Label every 5 minutes, and place tick marks between each 5-minute interval. Draw the hands of the clock based on the current time. Write the time next to the clock.

   a. If it is a quarter to 6 p.m., what time is it? ________
   b. Draw a clock that reads 7:57. Consider where the hour hand will be pointing at this time.

Extend Your Thinking

1. On the number line in Question 2B, above the tick marks where you labeled the drive to the café, lunch, and the drive back to work, draw clocks to represent the various times.

NAME:______________________________ DATE:______________

LESSON 4.1

Common Core Assessment Practice

Directions: Complete the problems below.

1. Mariah starts her piano lessons at 7:35 and finishes 22 minutes later. Draw a clock and add the hour and minute hand to show the time that Mariah finishes piano lessons.

2. Parker's horse riding lesson ended at 5:55 p.m. on Thursday. It lasted for 37 minutes. At what time did Parker's horse riding lesson begin? Create a number line to model your work.

3. Dana played in a soccer game that lasted 45 minutes. If the game started at 3:21 p.m., what time did it end?
   a. 4:06
   b. 4:05
   c. 2:56
   d. 4:20

4. How long did Fredrick ride his bike if he left his house at 9:23 a.m. and returned at 10:07 a.m.?
   a. 45 minutes
   b. 1 hour 47 minutes
   c. 47 minutes
   d. 44 minutes

LESSON 4.2

Volume and Mass

Common Core State Standards

- 3.MD.2

Mathematical Practices

- 1, 2, 4, 5, and 6

Estimated Time

- 60 minutes

Key Terms

- Volume
- Mass
- Graduated cylinder

Materials

- Lesson 4.2 Activity: Volume and Mass
- Lesson 4.2 Activity Sheet: Volume
- Lesson 4.2 Activity Sheet: Mass
- Lesson 4.2 Practice: Volume and Mass
- Lesson 4.2 Common Core Assessment Practice
- Various-sized containers
- Graduated cylinders
- Water
- Pan
- Kilogram bags of beans, rice, weights, or something similar
- Cups
- Beans
- Balance scales
- Mass weights
- Eye dropper

Objectives

In this lesson, students will:

- estimate and measure liquid volumes and masses, and
- utilize the four mathematical operations to solve real-world scenarios regarding volume and masses.

Lesson 4.2 Activity: Volume and Mass

In Part A of this activity, students will explore volume with a liter of water. The container needs to be easy to manage and pour by students. Provide each pair of students with 1 liter of water, along with a graduated cylinder that measures milliliters, and a container that is greater than 1 liter labeled Container A. Students will measure 100 ml of water in the graduated cylinder and then pour the water into Container A. Students then predict how many 100 ml measurements are in a liter (10). Students will check their predictions by continuing to measure, pour, and count the number of 100 ml measurements in the whole liter of water.

After exploring a liter of water, students will predict the volume of several containers. Provide each pair of students with four additional containers labeled B–E:

- Container B: half gallon,
- Container C: gallon,
- Container D: 1 liter (tall and narrow), and
- Container E: 1 liter (short and wide).

Students will predict and then measure the volume of each container. A pan can by used to catch any spilled water.

Next, students will explore mass in Part B of this activity. Students will work in pairs to find an object in the classroom they predict has a mass of 1 kilogram. Students are then provided with a 1 kg weight, such as a bag of beans, rice, or the like. Students will determine if the object they picked is greater than, less than, or approximately the same as the 1 kg weight. Students will then find other objects around the room they predict are 1 kilogram and use a balance scale with the object on one side and the 1 kg weight on the other. Grams will also be explored using the balance scale and weights to get an accurate, 100-gram measurement. Students will use the provided cup to predict and measure 100 grams of beans. Predictions will be made regarding how many 100-gram cups are in the kilogram bag of beans. Students then measure to test their predictions.

NAME:______________________________ DATE:______________

LESSON 4.2 ACTIVITY
Volume and Mass

Directions Part A: Recently, a manufacturing company had problems with the volume labels printed on their containers. You and a partner will work together to determine the amount of volume each container can hold in order to help create new labels.

Use the pan as a safety net to catch any spillage, because the company needs exact measurements. Measure 100 ml of water by pouring water from the liter container into the graduated cylinder. Estimate how many of the 100 ml measurements are in the liter container. Be sure to record your estimate on the Lesson 4.2 Activity Sheet: Volume handout. Test your predictions, using Container A to hold each 100 ml measurement of water you are able to obtain. Respond to the questions on Part I of the handout.

Continue with containers labeled B–E, by estimating how many liters of water each container can hold. Test your predictions. Be sure to keep record of your estimates and exact measurements on Part II of the handout.

Directions Part B: The company also asked that you predict the mass of various containers, but before you can create labels, you and a partner will explore mass. First, locate an item in the classroom that you predict has a mass of 1 kg and record the item on the Lesson 4.2 Activity Sheet: Mass handout. See how close your prediction was by using the 1 kg bag and the balance scale. Record the exact measurement of the item and see how close your prediction turned out to be! Using this new knowledge, locate other items around the classroom that you predict have a mass of 1 kg and test your predictions using the balance scale. Be sure to record your discoveries on Part I of the handout.

The company not only asked you to be prepared to label containers in kilograms, but also grams. Explore grams by pouring into a cup what you predict 100 g of beans would be. Test your prediction using the weights and balance scale. Once you have exactly 100 g of beans, mark the cup. Use the 100 g cup to determine how many 100 g there are in a kilogram. Be sure to answer the mass questions on Part II of the handout.

NAME:______________________________ DATE:______________

LESSON 4.2 ACTIVITY SHEET

Volume

Part I

1. Predict: How many 100 ml measurements are in 1 liter? ________

2. Exact measurement:
   a. How many 100 ml measurements are in 1 liter? ________
   b. Write a multiplication equation to help you solve how many total milliliters are in a liter. Use a variable to represent the unknown.

   c. How many milliliters are there in one liter? ________

Part II

1. Predict the volume of Containers B–E by circling your answer. Explain how you arrived at your predictions.

Container B =	< 1 liter	1 liter	$1\frac{1}{2}$ liters	close to 2 liters	> 3 liters
Container C =	< 1 liter	1 liter	$1\frac{1}{2}$ liters	close to 2 liters	> 3 liters
Container D =	< 1 liter	1 liter	$1\frac{1}{2}$ liters	close to 2 liters	> 3 liters
Container E =	< 1 liter	1 liter	$1\frac{1}{2}$ liters	close to 2 liters	> 3 liters

2. Measure and record your exact answers for the volume of Containers B–E. How close were your predictions?

Container B =	< 1 liter	1 liter	$1\frac{1}{2}$ liters	close to 2 liters	> 3 liters
Exact Volume:					
Container C =	< 1 liter	1 liter	$1\frac{1}{2}$ liters	close to 2 liters	> 3 liters
Exact Volume:					
Container D =	< 1 liter	1 liter	$1\frac{1}{2}$ liters	close to 2 liters	> 3 liters
Exact Volume:					
Container E =	< 1 liter	1 liter	$1\frac{1}{2}$ liters	close to 2 liters	> 3 liters
Exact Volume:					

NAME:_______________ DATE:_______________

LESSON 4.2 ACTIVITY SHEET

Mass

Part I

1. Prediction: What classroom object do you predict has a mass of 1 kg? ________

2. Exact answer: Is the item you predicted less than a kilogram, more than a kilogram, or approximately the same as a kilogram? ________

3. Fill in the table with the names of other objects you predict have a mass of 1 kg.

Item	Predicted Mass	Actual Mass (Circle your answer)
	1 kg	< 1 kg 1 kg >1 kg
	1 kg	< 1 kg 1 kg >1 kg
	1 kg	< 1 kg 1 kg >1 kg
	1 kg	< 1 kg 1 kg >1 kg
	1 kg	< 1 kg 1 kg >1 kg

Part II

1. How many 100 g cups did it take to fill the entire 1 kg? ________
   a. Write a multiplication equation to show how many grams are in a kilogram. Use a variable to represent the unknown.

   b. How many grams are in a kilogram? ________

Extend Your Thinking

1. Explore milliliters further. After seeing 100 ml in the graduated cylinder, make predictions about 1 ml of water. Use an eyedropper to visually see a milliliter of water.

2. Explore grams further. After seeing 100 g, make predictions about objects that have a mass of 1 g.

NAME:____ DATE:________________

Measurement and Data

LESSON 4.2 PRACTICE

Volume and Mass

1. You are in charge of making a punch for a party. The main ingredient is Sprite.
   a. The punch recipe calls for 3 liters of Sprite. If you tripled the recipe to make a larger batch, how many liters of Sprite would you need? ________

   b. If one person drinks about 100 ml of punch, how many people could drink 10 liters of punch? ________

2. A tennis shoe has a mass of about 1 kg.
   a. If there are 23 members in your class wearing tennis shoes, how many kilograms of tennis shoes are there? ________ Write an equation and solve.

   b. How many more children would you need to get a mass of 75 kg? ________ Explain your answer.

3. A container you found at the store has a volume of 7 liters. If you are filling a small pool and need 189 liters of water, how many times should you fill the 7-liter containers? ________ Write an equation and solve.

4. One of your friend's birthday presents has a mass of 27 kg. Each time one part of the present is removed, the mass decreases by 3 kg.
   a. How many pieces would have to be removed from the present to make it have a mass of 0 kg? ________

   b. If each part that is removed has more than 3 items, what can you say about the mass of each of the items?

5. A 2,675 g weight is placed in front of you. You are asked to change the label to represent both kilograms and grams.
   a. What would the label say?

   b. How many more grams would you need to have a 3 kg weight? ________

NAME:______________________________ DATE:______________

LESSON 4.2

Common Core Assessment Practice

Directions: Complete the problems below.

1. Which object's mass is closest to a kilogram?
   a. your desk
   b. clothespin
   c. dictionary
   d. pencil

2. Approximately how many liters of water do you think it would take to fill a bathroom sink?
   a. 15
   b. 3
   c. 1
   d. 12

3. Becky weighs 27 kilograms, and Tammy weighs 36 kilograms. How many more kilograms does Becky need to gain before she has the same mass as Tammy?
   a. 8
   b. 9
   c. 7
   d. 6

4. If a professional sportsman drinks 6 liters of water every day, how many liters of water will he drink in 4 weeks? Show your work.

5. If a recipe calls for 231 grams of salt and you have one bottle containing 79 grams, and another bottle that contains 115 grams of salt, how many more grams of salt do you need?

LESSON 4.3

Scaled Graphs

Common Core State Standards

- 3.MD.3

Mathematical Practices

- 1, 4, 6, and 7

Estimated Time

- 60 minutes

Key Terms

- Scaled graphs
- Data
- Pictograph
- Bar graph

Materials

- Lesson 4.3 Activity: Let's Graph It
- Lesson 4.3 Practice: Scaled Graphs
- Lesson 4.3 Common Core Assessment Practice
- Two sheets of poster paper per pair of students

Objectives

In this lesson, students will:

- collect data,
- organize data, and
- create scaled graphs to represent data.

Lesson 4.3 Activity: Let's Graph It

In this activity, students will work in small groups to collect data from their peers regarding a category of their choice, such as birth months or eye color. Students will need to decide on the best type of graph to display the data (pictograph or bar graph). A scale interval that best matches the collected data must be decided upon and displayed on the graphs. Students should provide reasoning for their interval choice. Data will be organized, and intervals will be decided after discussions between students.

NAME:________________________________ DATE:____________

LESSON 4.3 ACTIVITY

Let's Graph It

Directions: Complete the steps below.

How well do you know your classmates? It is time to get to know them even better. You will work with a small group to collect data regarding your peers. Choose a category, such as birth month, eye color, pets, or something else you are interested in, collect the data related to the category, organize the data, discuss and determine an appropriate interval and type of graph (pictograph or bar graph), and then graph the data. Compile the information below.

1. Determine what kind of data you will collect from your classmates. Write the category in the space below.

2. Organize the data in a meaningful way.
   a. Describe why you decided to group the data the way that you did.

   b. Is there a different way you could have categorized the data? If so, which way do you think would have been more beneficial?

3. Discuss with your group and determine which type of graph should be used (pictograph or bar graph) and decide on a scale interval. This should be based on the data.

4. How will you represent data that result in an odd number if the intervals are even numbered, or how will you represent data that result in an even number if the intervals represent an odd number?

5. Use the provided poster paper to create a pictograph or bar graph based on the collected data.

Extend Your Thinking

1. Collect data from your peers on a different topic that would result in the creation of a different type of graph than you previously created. Gather data that requires you to use intervals other than one.

NAME:______________________________ DATE:______________

LESSON 4.3 PRACTICE

Scaled Graphs

Which Hand Is It?

1. Use the graph below to answer the questions.

Right Handed	
Left Handed	

 = 2 students

a. How many students were asked if they were right handed or left handed? ________

b. $\frac{1}{4}$ of the students are ________ handed.

c. How many more students are right handed than left handed? ________

d. There are ________ times as many right-handed students as there are left handed.

2. Students were asked about their favorite type of music (see table below). After answering the questions, create a bar graph with the given data.

Type of Music	Number of Students
Classical	3
Folk	13
Country	18
Rock	9

a. Title the graph.
b. What should the intervals be for this graph? ________ Support your answer.

c. How many fewer people liked folk than country? ________

d. Out of the total number of students who were asked about their favorite type of music, how many did not choose rock? ________

e. Six times as many students chose country than what kind of music? ________

NAME:______________________________ DATE:______________

LESSON 4.3

Common Core Assessment Practice

1. You are responsible for creating a graph based on a survey. The results are below. If a bar graph were created, what should the intervals be? ________

9, 12, 3, 6, 7, 18

a. 2
b. 3
c. 4
d. 5

2. Classroom Accelerated Reading Points are presented below. Answer the questions based on the pictograph.

Mrs. Stacey's Class	□□□
Ms. Lin's Class	□□□□□□
Mr. Chase's Class	□□

□ = 3 books

a. How many more books did Ms. Lin's class read than Mrs. Stacey's and Mr. Chase's class combined? ________

b. How many books were read altogether? ________

c. How many more books did Ms. Lin's class read than Mrs. Stacey's? ________

3. Fill in the bar graph with the data provided.

# of students	Favorite Ice Cream			
20 16 12 8 4 0				
	Chocolate	Strawberry	Vanilla	Swirl
	Types of Ice Cream			

a. 17 students chose vanilla as their favorite ice cream.
b. Chocolate had 3 more students than vanilla.
c. Swirl had 10 votes.
d. No students chose strawberry as their favorite.

Measurement and Data

LESSON 4.4

Measurement Data

Common Core State Standards

- 3.MD.4

Mathematical Practices

- 4 and 5

Estimated Time

- 60 minutes

Key Terms

- Line plots

Materials

- Lesson 4.4 Activity: Length of Our Limbs
- Lesson 4.4 Practice: Measurement Data
- Lesson 4.4 Common Core Assessment Practice

Objectives

In this lesson, students will:

- generate data using measuring tools,
- create line plots based on generated data, and
- analyze line plots.

Lesson 4.4 Activity: Length of Our Limbs

In this activity, Partner A will measure certain parts of Partner B's body (right and left arm shoulder to elbow, right and left elbow to wrist, right and left wrist to fingertip, chin to top of forehead, and length of right foot and left foot) to the nearest $\frac{1}{4}$ inch. Measurements will be recorded, and then Partner B will measure Partner A to the nearest $\frac{1}{4}$ inch. The data obtained from the measurements will be placed on a class line plot for each measurement (or a sampling).

As a class, students will determine the shortest length and the longest length taken from the measurements, and those measurements will be the beginning and end of the line plot. Students will label each $\frac{1}{4}$ of an inch on the plot. For example, if the shortest length of one measurement was 3 inches and the longest was 5 inches, students would start the plot at 3 inches then label $3\frac{1}{4}$, $3\frac{1}{2}$, $3\frac{3}{4}$, 4, . . . until they reach 5 inches. Each pair of students would then share their measurements to complete the class plot.

NAME:______________________________ DATE:______________

LESSON 4.4 ACTIVITY

Length of Our Limbs

Directions: Complete the steps below.

Is your left side the same length as your right side? How do your limbs compare to the limbs of your classmates? Work with a partner to measure each other to the nearest $\frac{1}{4}$ inch and determine the proportionality of your body! Record the specific measurements for each other in the spaces below. With your partner, determine who will be Partner A and who will be Partner B.

1. Partner A: Measure Partner B to the nearest $\frac{1}{4}$ inch and record the measurements.

Partner A's Measurements

- Right arm: shoulder to elbow _______
- Left arm: shoulder to elbow _______
- Right elbow to wrist _______
- Left elbow to wrist _______
- Right wrist to fingertip _______
- Left wrist to fingertip _______
- Chin to top of forehead _______
- Length of right foot _______
- Length of left foot _______

2. Partner B: Measure Partner A to the nearest $\frac{1}{4}$ inch and record the measurements.

Partner B's Measurements

- Right arm: shoulder to elbow _______
- Left arm: shoulder to elbow _______
- Right elbow to wrist _______
- Left elbow to wrist _______
- Right wrist to fingertip _______
- Left wrist to fingertip _______
- Chin to top of forehead _______
- Length of right foot _______
- Length of left foot _______

3. The class will now create line plots to display all of these data. As a class, decide the starting and ending points. Then use a ruler to make a tick mark every $\frac{1}{4}$ of an inch. Label the line plot with the measurements, a label for the measurements, and a title for each one that was taken (for example, right elbow to wrist, left elbow to wrist).

4. How many measurements were greater than 9 inches? ________

5. Develop three questions that another group of students could answer by looking at your line plot.

Extend Your Thinking

1. Think of a time when a line plot might be useful, other than measuring the length of body parts. What type of information is best displayed in a line plot?

NAME:______________________________ DATE:______________

LESSON 4.4 PRACTICE

Measurement Data

Directions: Complete the problems below.

1. Science students were measuring the distance various marbles roll. Use the data provided in the line plot below to answer the questions.

Marble Roll

2	$2\frac{1}{4}$	$2\frac{1}{2}$	$2\frac{3}{4}$	3	$3\frac{1}{4}$	$3\frac{1}{2}$	$3\frac{3}{4}$	4	$4\frac{1}{4}$	$4\frac{1}{2}$	$4\frac{3}{4}$	5
	X X	X			X X X	X X	X X		X X			X X

(inches the marbles rolled)

   a. The marbles that rolled the shortest distance rolled $2\frac{1}{4}$ inches. The marbles that rolled the farthest distance rolled 5 inches. How many more fourths were between the shortest and longest roll? ________

   b. How many more marbles that rolled more than 3 inches were there than marbles that rolled less than 3 inches? ________

2. Students measured the height of all of the students in their class. Use the data in the table to create a line plot on a separate piece of paper and answer the questions.

Student	Height	Student	Height
A	48 in.	H	$48\frac{1}{4}$ in.
B	$48\frac{1}{4}$ in.	I	$48\frac{1}{4}$ in.
C	47 in.	J	$48\frac{3}{4}$ in.
D	$46\frac{1}{4}$ in.	K	$48\frac{1}{2}$ in.
E	$46\frac{1}{2}$ in.	L	$48\frac{3}{4}$ in.
F	$48\frac{3}{4}$ in.	M	48 in.
G	48 in.	N	$48\frac{1}{4}$ in.

a. How many fourths of an inch taller are the tallest children compared to the shortest children? ________

b. How many full inches taller are the tallest children compared to the shortest children? ________

c. How many fourths are left over after determining the number of full inches? ________

d. How much taller are the tallest children than the children with the most common height? ________

Extend Your Thinking

1. Number 2 describes data collection by a different class. Conduct the same research on your own class by measuring the height of every student and record the data in either a line plot or a graph of your choice.

NAME:____ DATE:____________________

Measurement and Data

LESSON 4.4

Common Core Assessment Practice

Directions: Complete the problems below.

1. About how long is an unsharpened pencil?
   - **a.** 8 inches
   - **b.** 8 yards
   - **c.** 2 meters
   - **d.** 1 kilometer

2. Use your ruler to measure the length of the shape below. Measure to the nearest $\frac{1}{4}$ inch. What is the length? ________

3. The frame for a picture you want to hang on the wall requires a nail that is between 3 inches and $3\frac{1}{2}$ inches. What length nail should you use?
   - **a.** $3\frac{3}{4}$ in.
   - **b.** $\frac{3}{3}$ in.
   - **c.** $3\frac{1}{4}$ in.
   - **d.** 3 in.

4. A new sticker that you received for your bedroom wall measures $4\frac{1}{4}$ inches. If you only have a space on the wall that is $2\frac{3}{4}$ inches, how many fourths do you need to trim from the sticker so that it will fit? Explain your answer.

LESSON 4.5

Area

Common Core State Standards

- 3.MD.5
- 3.MD.6

Mathematical Practices

- 1, 2, 4, 5, and 6

Estimated Time

- 60 minutes

Key Terms

- Area
- Plane figure

Materials

- Lesson 4.5 Activity: Floor Plans
- Lesson 4.5 Practice: Area
- Lesson 4.5 Common Core Assessment Practice
- Centimeter grid paper printed on transparent paper
- Centimeter grid paper
- Colored paper premeasured and cut out for the practice

Objectives

In this lesson, students will:

- analyze figures to determine area, and
- recognize area as an attribute of a plane figure.

Lesson 4.5 Activity: Floor Plans

In this activity, students will determine the area of various rooms within a house and then provide layout options for that room, representing the same area. Students will first be given three layouts for a utility room in which they will have to determine the area by laying a transparent centimeter grid sheet on top of the three layouts. Students will count the grid to determine the area. After students practice and recognize that area is an attribute of plane figures, and once they understand what a square unit is, students will create various layouts for multiple rooms in the house with the same area by using grid paper. Students can count to determine the area and use a pencil to outline the various layouts. Students should determine as many different rectangular shapes as they can with the given area. If students struggle, review factors.

NAME:____ DATE:______________

LESSON 4.5 ACTIVITY

Floor Plans

Directions: Being an architect requires you to complete calculations and often give advice to your customers. You have been hired by a client to create a layout of various rooms for her house. Be prepared to give your professional opinion as to which layout would be the best for which rooms within the home. You will begin by using the transparent grid paper to determine the area of the utility room options. Then, you will help determine the layout options for the backyard, hallway, and kitchen.

1. Using any method you wish, determine the area of utility room floor plan options.
   a. Figure A area: ________
   b. Figure B area: ________
   c. Figure C area: ________

Figure A

Figure B

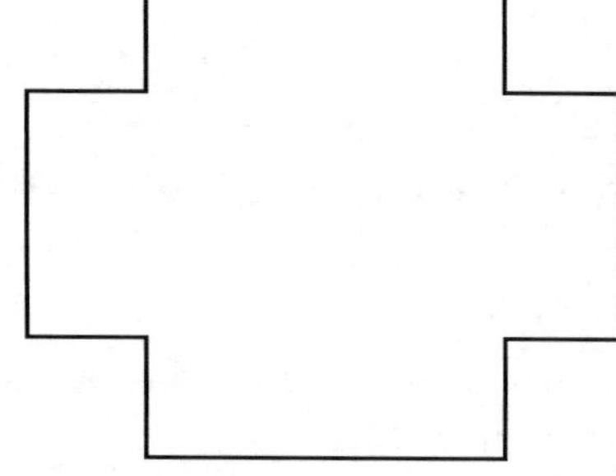

Figure C

2. Explain the method you used and explain its accuracy.

3. On the provided grid paper, count and outline as many rectangular backyard layouts you can create with an area of 15 square centimeters.
   a. How do you know you have created all of the shapes with an area of 15 square centimeters?

   b. A backyard with length of 1 cm and a width of 15 has the same area but looks different than a yard with a length of 15 cm and a width of 1 cm. Discuss and explain why the area is the same.

4. Use the grid paper to create as many rectangular hallways as possible with an area of 18 square centimeters.
   a. Which layout would be the best option for a hallway? Think about the purposes of hallways.

5. Create as many options for a rectangular kitchen with an area of 32 square centimeters as possible.
   a. Which kitchen layout would you recommend to your customer and why?

Extend Your Thinking

1. Remember, perimeter is the distance all the way around a figure. Calculate the perimeter of each layout and discuss your findings with a partner. Do all of the created layout options have the same perimeter? Why or why not?

NAME:________________________ DATE:____________

LESSON 4.5 PRACTICE

Area

Directions: Complete the problems below.

1. Using scratch paper and any method you desire, create two rectangles with the following measurements. Label the figures with the length, width, and area measurements.
   a. Figure 1: 8 x 8
   b. Figure 2: 17 x 5

2. On the provided grid paper, shade as many rectangular shapes as you can with an area of 24 square centimeters. How do you know you have created all of the possible rectangular options?

3. If the area of a figure is 22 square meters, what are some possible options for the number of square meters in one row?

4. What can you say about the size and shape of figures that have the same area but look different?

5. Imagine that Figure 2 in Question 1 is a nonrectangular layout for a utility room. Other than counting the grid squares, how could you determine the area of nonrectangular shapes?

Extend Your Thinking

1. Using the transparent grid paper and the equilateral triangles below, think about how you could determine the area and perimeter of triangles.

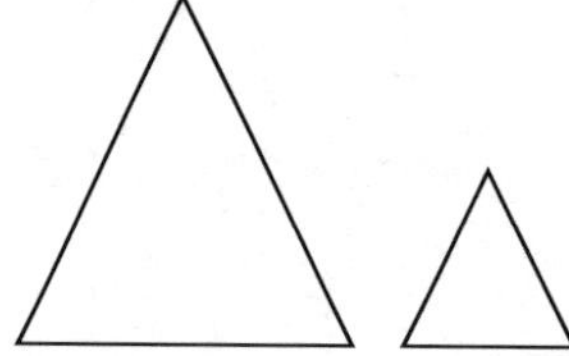

NAME:______________________________ DATE:______________

LESSON 4.5

Common Core Assessment Practice

Directions: Complete the problems below.

1. Justin placed 7 dots in the rectangle. About how many total dots will it take to cover the rectangle?

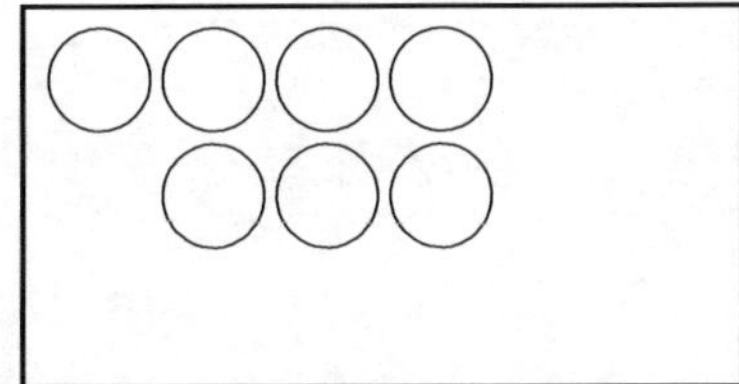

   a. about 26
   b. about 4
   c. about 18
   d. about 32

2. You are trying to lay black and white checkered tiles on your bathroom floor. The bathroom has a measurement of 6 feet by 9 feet. What units will you use to determine how much tile you need?
   a. Square feet
   b. Cubic feet
   c. Yards
   d. Inches

3. If you were in charge of building a house, list three circumstances in which you would have to determine the area of a location in the house. Explain why finding the area would be necessary.

LESSON 4.6

Area and Multiplication

Common Core State Standards

- 3.MD.7a
- 3.MD.7b

Mathematical Practices

- 1, 2, 4, 5, and 6

Estimated Time

- 60 minutes

Key Terms

- Tiling
- Rectangle
- Factor

Materials

- Lesson 4.6 Activity: Area and Multiplication
- Lesson 4.6: Rectangles (copy these on cardstock and cut before lesson)
- Lesson 4.6 Practice: Area and Multiplication
- Lesson 4.6 Common Core Assessment Practice
- Grid paper

Objectives

In this lesson, students will:

- tile figures to determine the relationship between tiling and multiplying when solving for area, and
- utilize multiplication skills to determine area.

Lesson 4.6 Activity: Area and Multiplication

In this activity, students will estimate the size of rectangles based on their area by placing them in order from least to greatest. Students will use Lesson 4.6 Rectangles, which have been measured in centimeters and labeled with an L for length and a W for width. The rectangles have the following measurements with the length listed first: 8 x 5, 3 x 11, 4 x 2, 8 x 4, 1 x 6, and 11 x 4. Once students have placed them in order, they will check their work by sketching a grid onto the rectangles. Students should be made aware that the rectangles have been measured using square inches. After grids are sketched, students will use rulers to measure the length and width, correct the grid, and determine the area of each rectangle. Students will then make any corrections to the order of the rectangles.

NAME:______________________________ DATE:______________

LESSON 4.6 ACTIVITY

Area and Multiplication

Directions: Often, the sizes of various shapes are tricky on our eyes. Items that look relatively smaller than other items often have the same or more area than the others. Let's see if shapes play tricks on your eyes or if you can estimate the area of shapes without any mathematical tools. You and a partner will work together to complete the steps below.

1. Place the rectangles in order from least to greatest.

2. Estimate the area of each rectangle using any method you wish. Write the estimated area on the rectangles. Describe the method you used and why such method was appropriate.

3. Use a centimeter ruler to measure and find the exact length and width of each rectangle. Make any corrections necessary on the grid. Measure and record the exact area of each rectangle. Rearrange the rectangles if needed from least to greatest.

Extend Your Thinking

1. On the other side of the rectangles, determine the area if it had been measured in square inches. Estimate to draw the grid and then use a ruler to measure and determine the area. How does the area measured in centimeters compare to the area when measured in inches?

NAME:______________________________ DATE:______________

LESSON 4.6

Rectangles

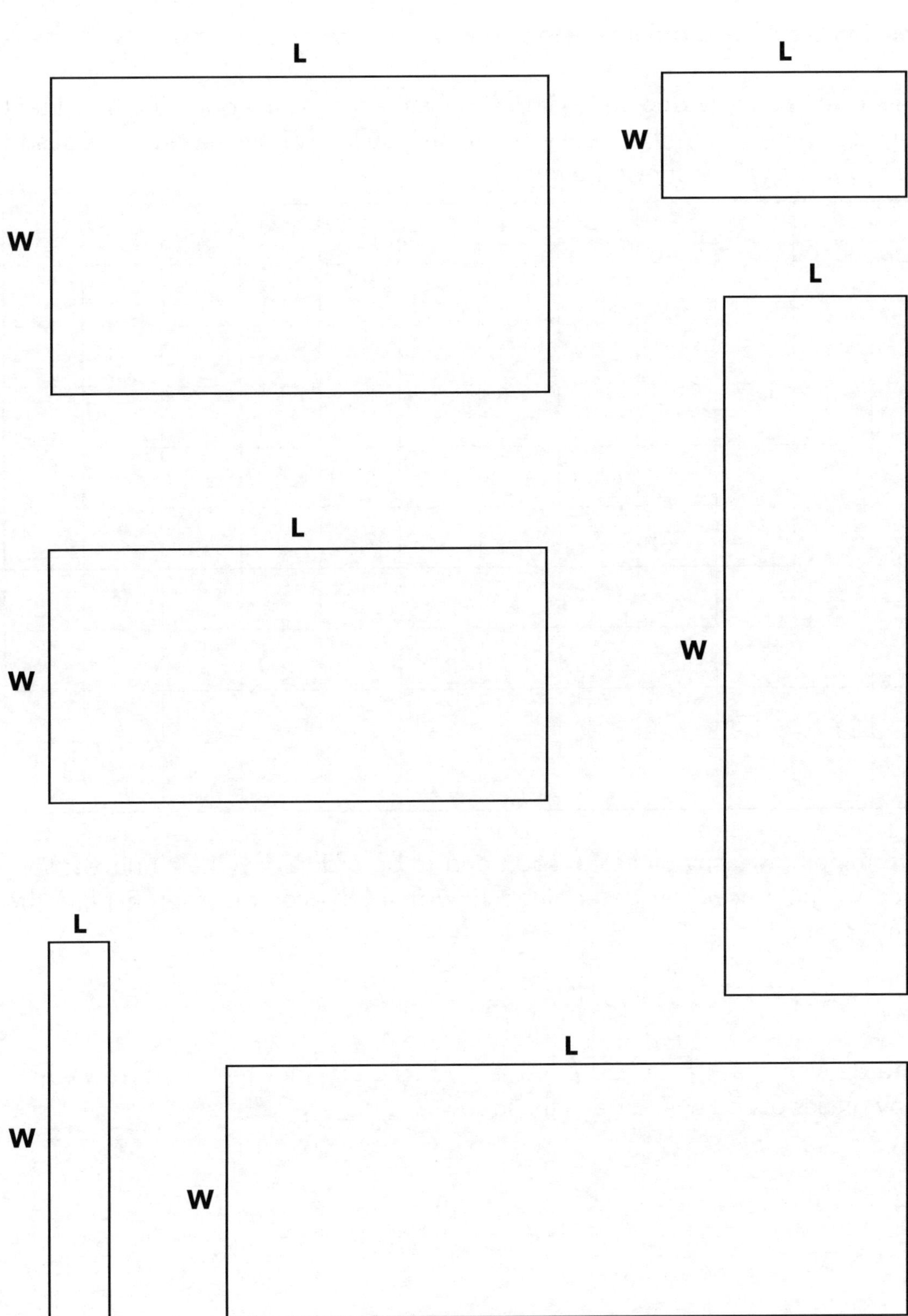

Measurement and Data

NAME:______________________________ DATE:______________

LESSON 4.6 PRACTICE

Area and Multiplication

Directions: Complete the problems below.

1. During the summer, you decide to landscape yards for extra money. It is important that you determine the area of each yard so that you know how many pieces of sod to order. The first yard is shown below.

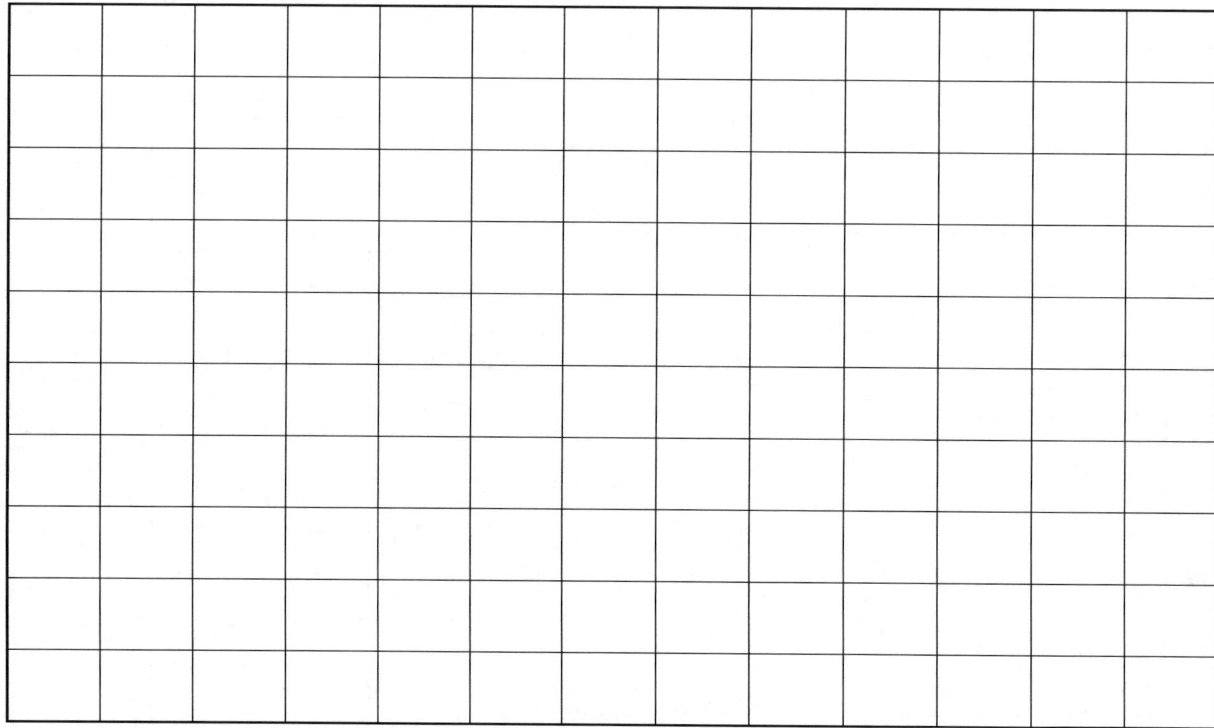

   a. Determine how many pieces of sod need to be ordered. Write a number sentence to show how you determined how many pieces to order. Explain the number sentence.

   b. If the delivery truck only had enough sod to place into the first 5 rows, how many pieces of sod would be in these rows? ________

2. For the next yard, you just received an order slip that said 72 square feet of grass were needed.
   a. Use grid paper to determine what the yard could look like if it had an area of 72 square feet.
   b. What is the most number of rows the yard could possibly have? ________
   c. In this case, how many square feet would be in each row? ________

3. The area of the third yard you were asked to landscape was determined by skip counting.

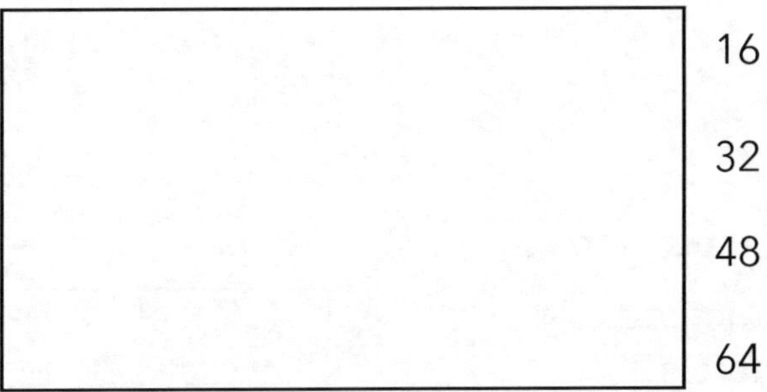

   a. Based on the picture, how many square yards were in each row? ________
   b. What would the repeated addition sentence be if addition was used to solve for the area?
   c. What is the multiplication equation that represents the picture?

4. The fourth yard is 6 square feet wide and 13 square feet long. Draw a grid to represent the data. What is the area of the yard? ________

5. If you were paid $7 per square unit for each yard, how much more money did you make on the fourth yard than on the third yard? ________

6. Do you feel it is more efficient to solve area problems by counting square units, using repeated addition, or multiplying? Support your answer.

NAME:______________________________ DATE:____________

LESSON 4.6

Common Core Assessment Practice

Directions: Complete the problems below.

1. Our class wants to build a rose garden with an area of 48 square feet. Which of the following does not show a possible size of the garden?
   a. 48 feet x 2 feet
   b. 24 feet x 2 feet
   c. 1 foot x 48 feet
   d. 6 feet x 8 feet

2. What is the area of the shaded portion?
   a. 20 square centimeters
   b. 2 square centimeters
   c. 6 square centimeters
   d. 9 square centimeters

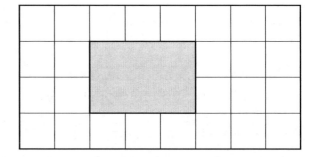

3. What multiplication equation could be used to solve for the area of Number 2? Explain how you knew each factor.

4. Draw a different shaped rectangle with the same area as the one above. Explain why your drawing is equivalent to the other.

Measurement and Data

LESSON 4.7

Area and Addition

Common Core State Standards

- 3.MD.7c
- 3.MD.7d

Mathematical Practices

- 1, 2, 4, and 5

Estimated Time

- 60 minutes

Key Terms

- Distributive property
- Decompose
- Rectilinear

Objectives

In this lesson, students will:

- represent the distributive property through area models, and
- decompose rectilinear figures to solve for the area.

Materials

- Lesson 4.7 Activity: Area and Addition
- Lesson 4.7 Area and Addition Cards (copy these on cardstock and cut before lesson)
- Lesson 4.7 Practice: Area and Addition
- Lesson 4.7 Common Core Assessment Practice

Lesson 4.7 Activity: Area and Addition

In this activity, students will be given the layout of three tree houses on three different cards. Certain lengths and widths will be given, along with the area of specific rooms. Students will determine the area of each room by decomposing the figure. The rooms will be labeled once the measurements have been discovered.

NAME:______________________________ DATE:______________

LESSON 4.7 ACTIVITY

Area and Addition

Directions: Knowing the measurement of each room in a tree house is essential when laying floors and decorating. Help determine the area of rooms within the three tree houses by decomposing figures. Follow the steps below.

With your partner, choose one card at a time. The measurements of the rooms have been given. Decompose the figure to solve for the area of each section, and use the information provided to label each room of the house.

1. **a.** Label the following rooms on the first card, Tree House 1.
   - The living room is 96 square feet. Label the living room.
   - The bedroom is 24 square feet. Label the bedroom.
   - The kitchen is 8 square feet. Label the kitchen.
   - The dining room is 8 square feet. Label the dining room.
   - The hallway is 12 square feet. Label the hallway.

   b. What is the total area of the entire house?

2. **a.** Label the following rooms on the second card, Tree House 2.
   - Two porches are each 2 square feet. Label the two porches.
   - The foyer is 1 square foot. Label the foyer.
   - The hallway is 3 square feet. Label the hallway.
   - The bedroom is 6 square feet. Label the bedroom.
   - The kitchen is 16 square feet. Label the kitchen.
   - The dining room is 8 square feet. Label the dining room.
   - The utility room is 4 square feet. Label the utility room.
   - The sunroom is 3.5 square feet. Label the sunroom.

   b. What is the total area of the second house?

3. **a.** Label the following rooms on the third card, Tree House 3.
   - The hallway is 4 square feet. Label the hallway.
   - The playroom is 20 square feet. Label the playroom.
   - The living room is 12 square feet. Label the living room.

   b. What is the total area of the third home?

NAME:______________________________ DATE:______________

LESSON 4.7

Area and Addition Cards

Tree House 1

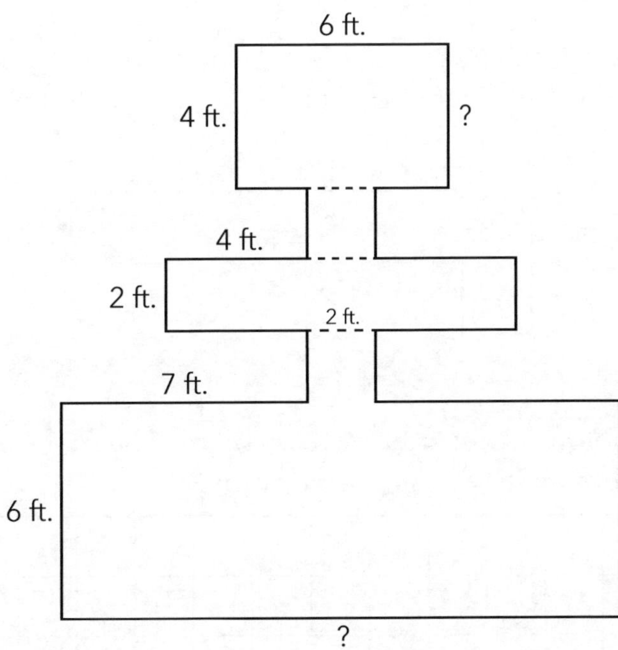

Tree House 2

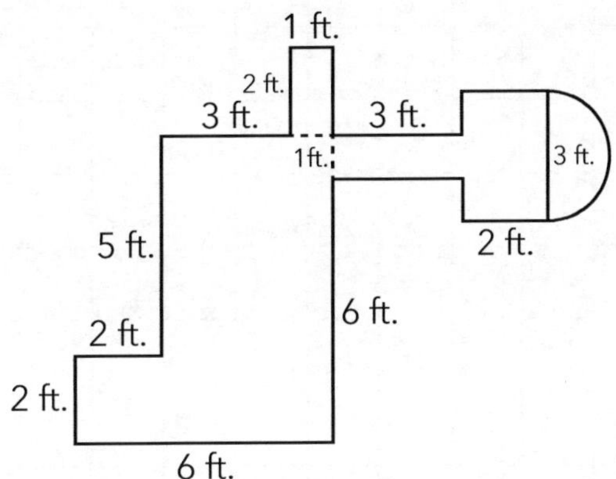

Tree House 3

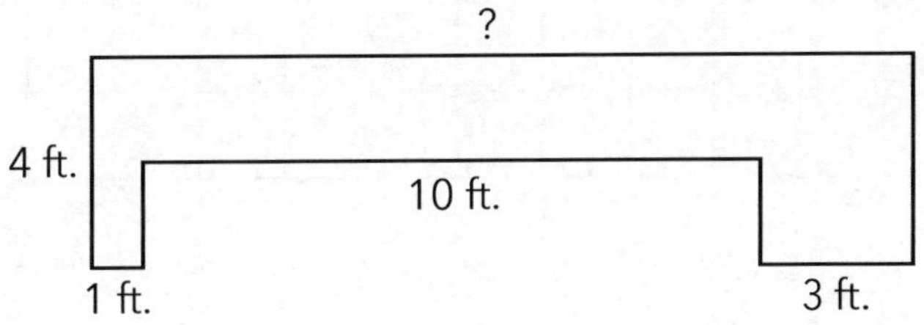

NAME:______________________________ DATE:______________

LESSON 4.7 PRACTICE

Area and Addition

Directions: Complete the problems below.

1. The area of the local bakery is unknown. Use the drawing to determine the total area of the building. What is the total area? ________

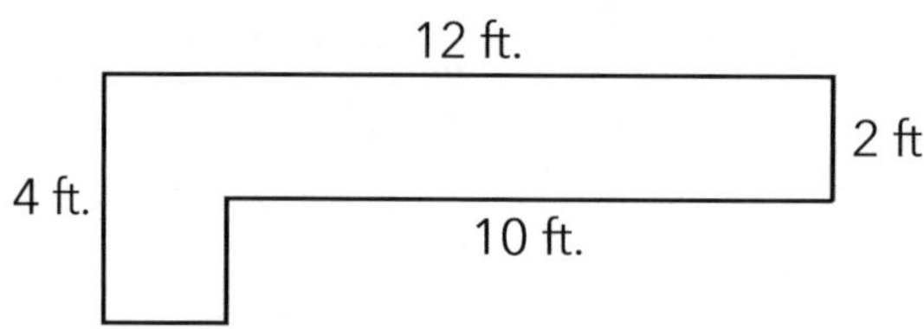

2. The entire area below represents 14 rows of 14. Shade 14 rows of 4. What is the multiplication equation for the shaded portion?

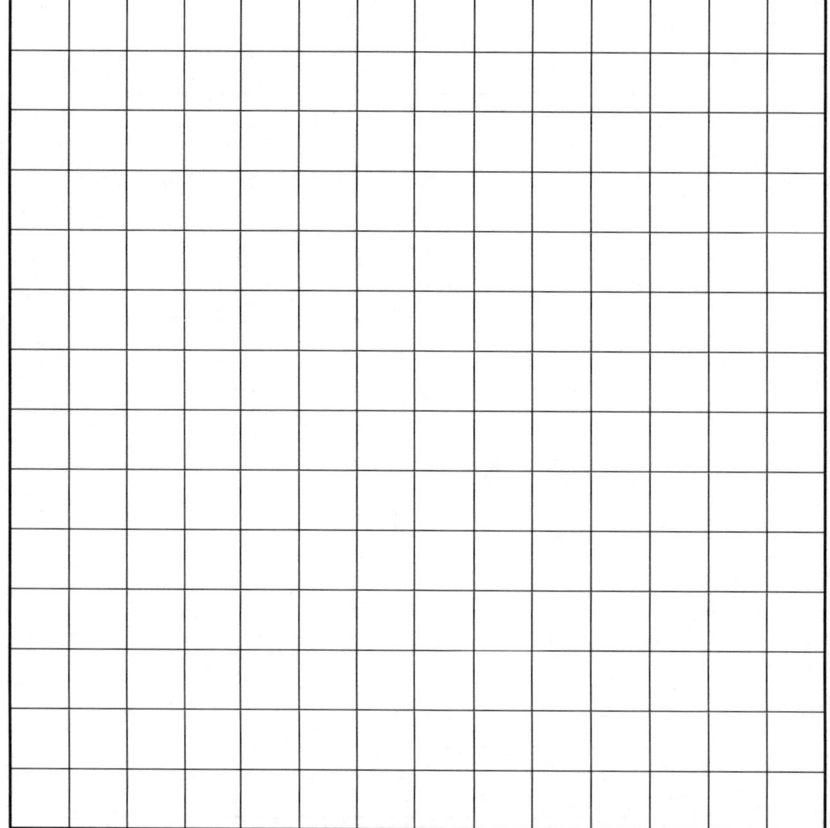

3. What is the multiplication equation for the nonshaded portion?

4. Using the same figure, show how addition can be used to add the two smaller figures to solve for the area of the larger figure.

5. How else could you decompose the array?

6. Decompose the following figure by shading and adding to determine the area.

NAME:______________________________ DATE:______________

LESSON 4.7

Common Core Assessment Practice

Directions: Complete the problems below.

1. Find the area of the shaded figure. Include the scale.

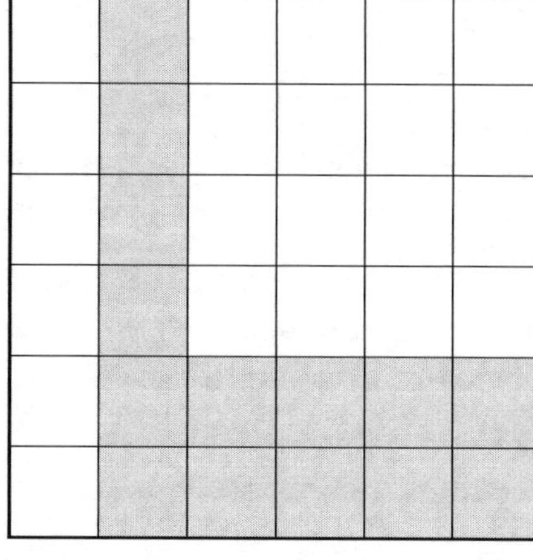

2. Use the picture above to answer the following questions.
   a. Is this the only way to decompose the shaded figure into two different rectangles? ________ If not, what are the other multiplication equations can be used to describe the decomposition?

   b. Show how addition of the two multiplication equations will result in the area of the shaded figure.

3. Which number sentence best describes the area of the nonshaded and shaded square?
   a. $6 \times 6 = (4 + 6) + (6 + 2)$
   b. $6 \times 6 = 6(6 \times 6)$
   c. $6 \times 6 = (4 \times 6) + (2 \times 6)$
   d. $6 \times 6 = 10 + 8$

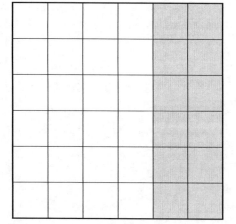

4. Use a ruler to draw a figure with an area of 11 square inches. Be sure the figure is made of several rectangles.

a. What is the multiplication equation for each of the rectangles?

b. Show how adding the area of each smaller rectangle will result in the 11 square inch area of the entire figure.

LESSON 4.8

Perimeter of Polygons

Common Core State Standards

- 3.MD.8

Mathematical Practices

- 1, 4, and 7

Estimated Time

- 60 minutes

Key Terms

- Perimeter
- Polygon

Materials

- Lesson 4.8 Activity: Polygon Perimeter
- Lesson 4.8 Practice: Perimeter of Polygons
- Lesson 4.8 Common Core Assessment Practice
- Unifix Cubes
- Grid paper

Objectives

In this lesson, students will:

- solve for the perimeter of polygons, and
- create polygons based on given perimeter information.

Lesson 4.8 Activity: Polygon Perimeter

In this activity, students will work together to figure out various layouts for swimming pools based on given data. Unifix Cubes (each representing 1 square foot) will be used to create the pools. Students will sketch the shape of the pool created by the cubes onto a sheet of paper and then label each side based on the number of cubes. As students build the various options for each pool based on the data given, a chart will be filled in for students to discover patterns once all of the pools are complete.

NAME:__________ DATE:__________

LESSON 4.8 ACTIVITY

Polygon Perimeter

Directions: The only thing better than swimming in a pool is being the person who is trusted to design the pool! You and a partner will use the Unifix Cubes to build swimming pools based on the given information. Each cube will represent one square foot. Provide a sketch of each pool with labeled measurements based on the number of cubes used. Be sure to fill in the chart after you build each pool.

1. Your first swimming pool client is undecided about the shape of the pool, but he does know that the area must be 100 square feet.
   a. Build, sketch, and record some of the measurement possibilities for the swimming pool.

Length	Width	Area	Perimeter
		100 sq. ft.	
		100 sq. ft.	
		100 sq. ft.	
		100 sq. ft.	
		100 sq. ft.	
		100 sq. ft.	
		100 sq. ft.	
		100 sq. ft.	

b. You then learned that the perimeter of the pool must be less than 150 feet. Which pool options have a perimeter less than 150 feet?

c. Would the pool with the largest perimeter be the best option for the client who has a family of four children, plus himself and his wife, who love to swim and play? Why or why not?

2. Your next pool client is requesting a pool with a perimeter of 48 feet.
   a. If you drew five possibilities for a pool with a perimeter of 48 feet, using the smallest whole number side lengths, would the area of the pools be the same? Why or why not?

   b. Build, sketch, and record the measurements of five rectangular possibilities for the swimming pool. Whole numbers or half numbers can be used.

   c. Based on your possibilities, which pool has the largest swimming area?

3. Use the table to answer the questions.

Length	Width	Area	Perimeter
8 ft.			48 ft.
			48 ft.
			48 ft.
			48 ft.
			48 ft.

   a. If the length was 8 feet, what would the width be? ________ How many square feet would the area be? ________

Measurement and Data

b. Based on the information in the table, complete the generalization:
As the length gets longer and the width gets shorter, . . .

c. Is this always true? What if the length was 12 feet and the width was 12 feet? Would the pattern in the table still hold true? ________

d. If the perimeter has to be 48 feet, then the maximum length of the pool could only be how long? ________

Extend Your Thinking

1. Create a pool layout that is rectilinear and made of several rectangles with a perimeter of 52 centimeters. What is the area of the pool? ________

2. Design several pools with a perimeter of 36 feet. Which pool design would be best for teaching swimming lessons to young children? ________

NAME:____ DATE:________________

LESSON 4.8 PRACTICE

Perimeter of Polygons

Directions: Complete the problems below.

1. What is the perimeter of the pentagon below?

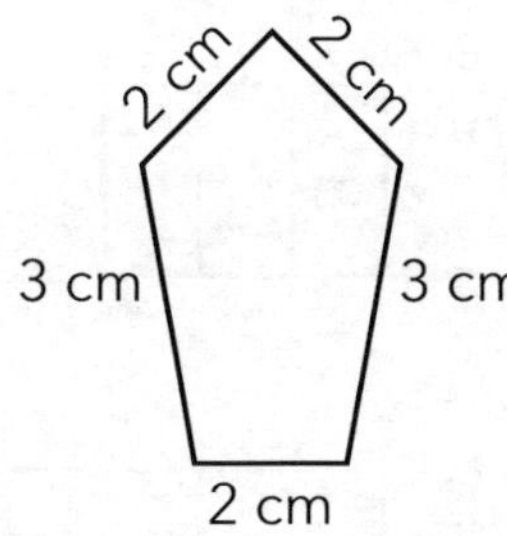

2. The following rectangle has a perimeter of 78 inches. Label each side.

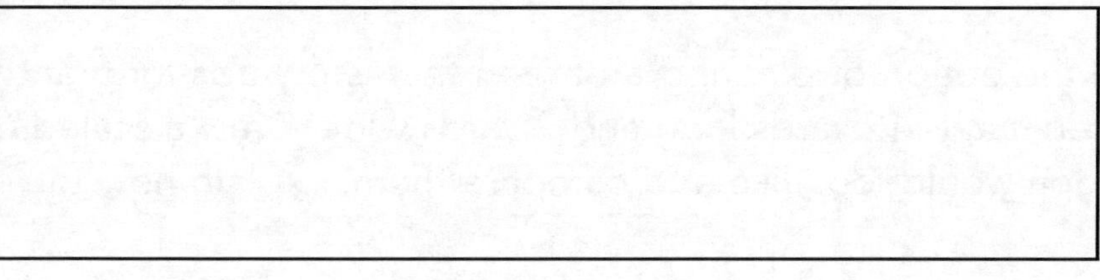

3. What is the area of the above rectangle? ________

4. Use grid paper to draw a rectangle with a perimeter of 52 cm. Draw a second rectangle with a perimeter of 52 cm, but be sure the two rectangles have a different area.

5. Timothy was absent from school and missed a lesson about perimeter. Explain to Timothy how you can determine the length of each side of a rectangle, even if you only know the length of one side (71 in.) and the total perimeter (148 in.). Be sure to provide Timothy with an example along with the explanation.

NAME:______________________________ DATE:______________

LESSON 4.8

Common Core Assessment Practice

Directions: Complete the problems below.

1. Each square tile has a side that is 1 inch long. Which figure has a perimeter of 10 inches?

   a. 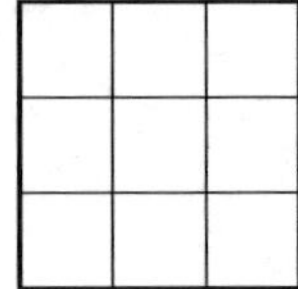

   b. 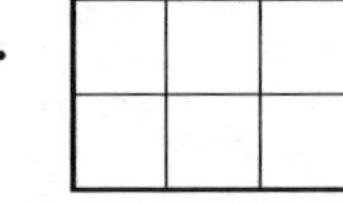

   c. 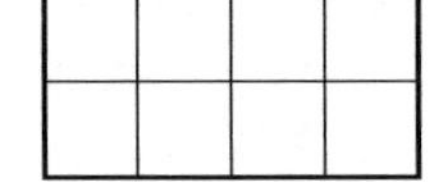

   d. 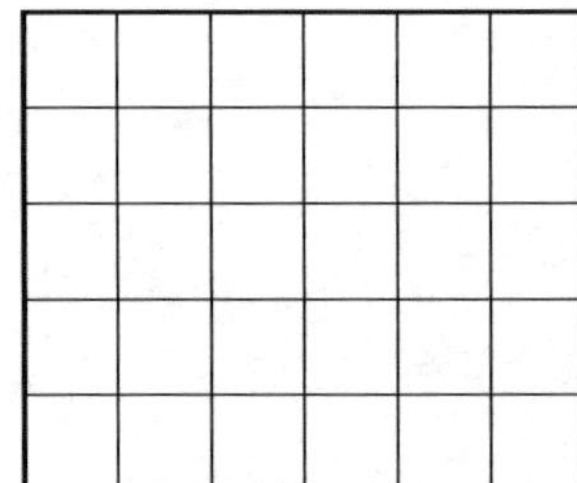

2. You have the option of planting a garden that is 6 yards long and 4 yards wide or a garden that is 12 yards long and 2 yards wide. Draw a scaled model of what each garden would look like and compare them. Explain how they are alike and different.

3. Which measurements would result in the same area but different perimeter?

   a. Figure 1: 5 x 4 Figure 2: 6 x 3

   b. Figure 1: 7 x 4 Figure 2: 9 x 3

   c. Figure 1: 6 x 5 Figure 2: 5 x 6

   d. Figure 1: 6 x 4 Figure 2: 8 x 3

4. In order for a figure to have the same area, but different perimeter, the figures must:
   a. have lengths and widths that are equal.
   b. have lengths and widths that are factors of the same number.
   c. have equivalent sides.
   d. have same length sides, but different widths.

SECTION V

Geometry

LESSON 5.1

Classifying Shapes

Common Core State Standards

- 3.G.1

Mathematical Practices

- 5, 6, and 7

Estimated Time

- 60 minutes

Key Terms

- Attributes
- Categorize
- Subcategories

Materials

- Lesson 5.1 Activity: Classifying Shapes
- Lesson 5.1 Shapes (copy these on cardstock and cut before lesson)
- Lesson 5.1 Practice: Classifying Shapes
- Lesson 5.1 Common Core Assessment Practice
- Bag for shapes

Objectives

In this lesson, students will:

- classify shapes based on attributes, and
- identify shapes to categorize them in categories and subcategories.

Lesson 5.1 Activity: Classifying Shapes

In this activity, students will classify shapes in Venn diagrams on the handout using various shapes. After all of the shapes have been placed in the first Venn diagram, and the students agree, then sketches will be made of each shape on the Venn diagram for grading purposes. Students will continue using the same shapes to complete the subsequent diagrams on the handout.

NAME:______________________________ DATE:______________

LESSON 5.1 ACTIVITY

Classifying Shapes

Directions: Shapes are all around us, and some shapes are even made up of other shapes. You and a partner will work together to classify shapes. Use the bag of shapes and sort them into different categories in each Venn diagram below. Then, sketch the shapes on the cards onto the Venn diagram. Be sure to answer the questions that follow each diagram.

1. Fill in the labeled Venn diagram with the correct shapes.

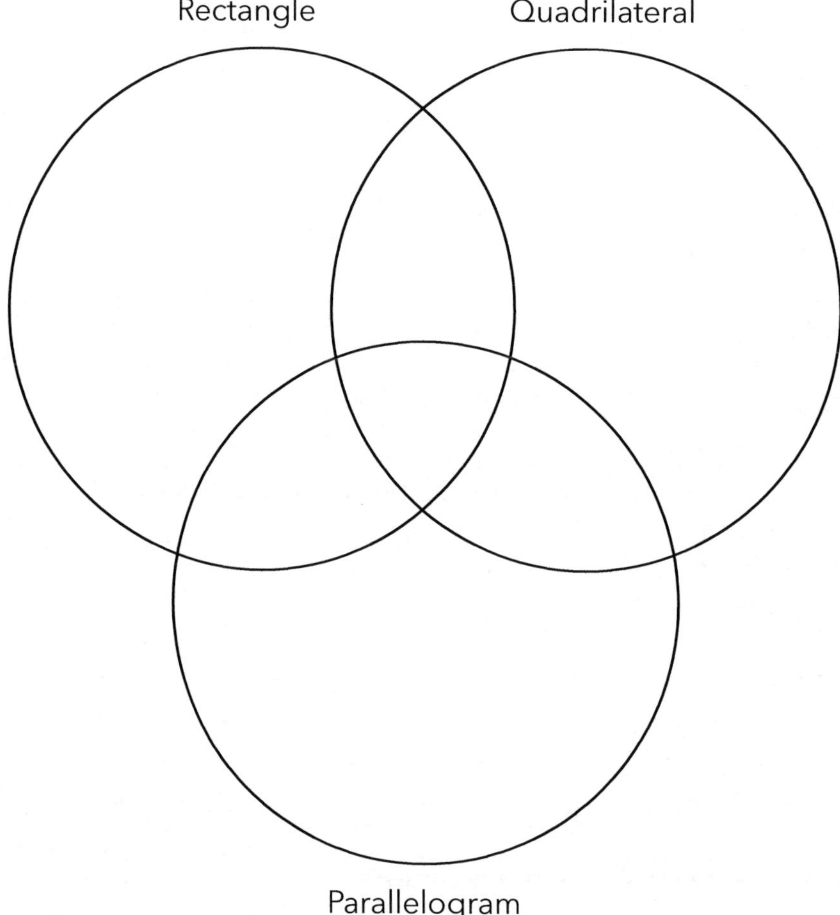

2. What generalization can you make about parallelograms after completing this Venn diagram?

3. Fill in the Venn diagram with the correct shapes.

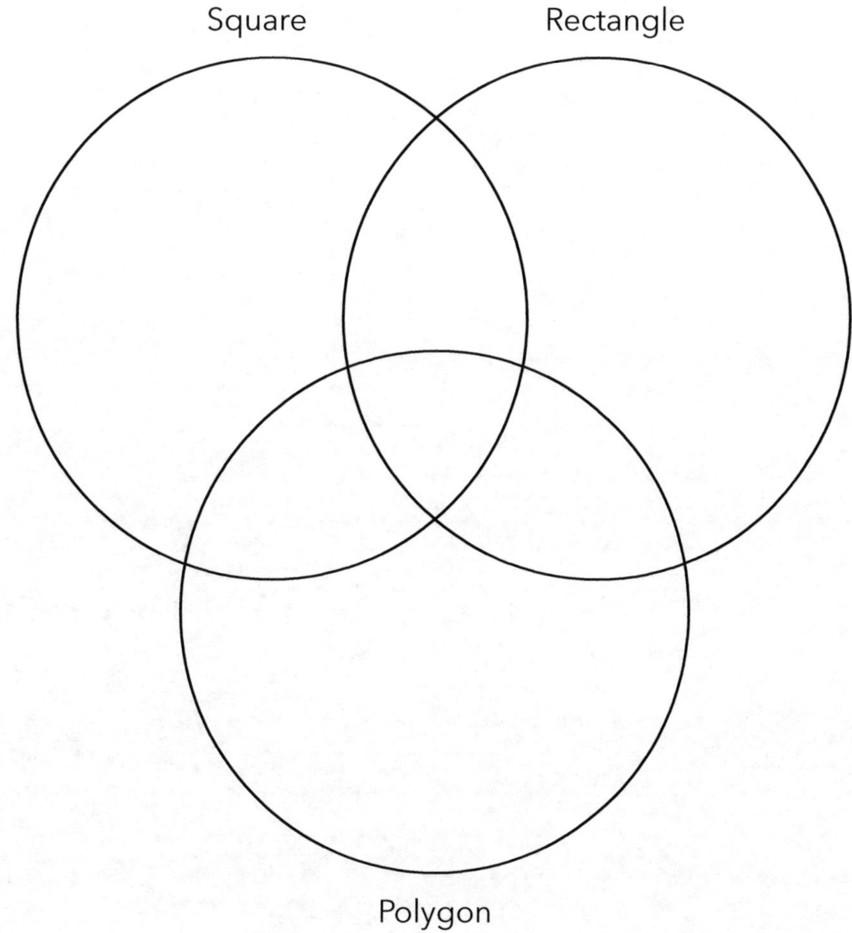

4. Of the provided shapes, which is the only one to be classified as a square, rectangle, and a polygon?

5. Fill in the Venn diagram with the correct shapes.

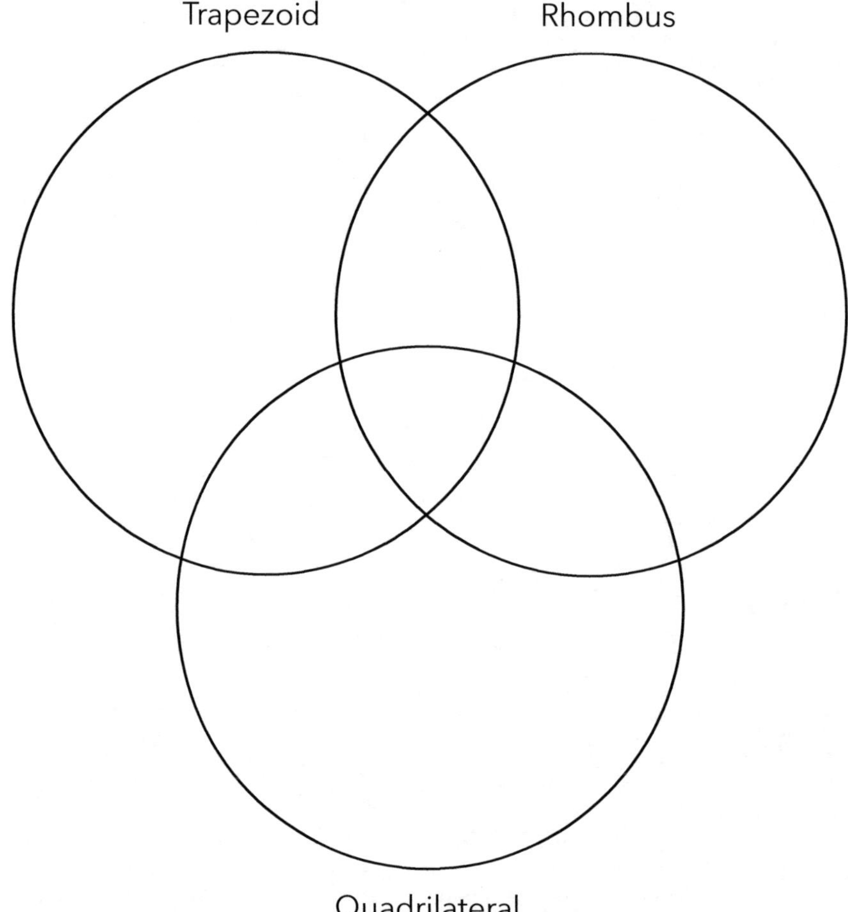

6. Explain why none of the shapes fall in the center of the Venn diagram.

7. Fill in the Venn diagram with the correct shapes.

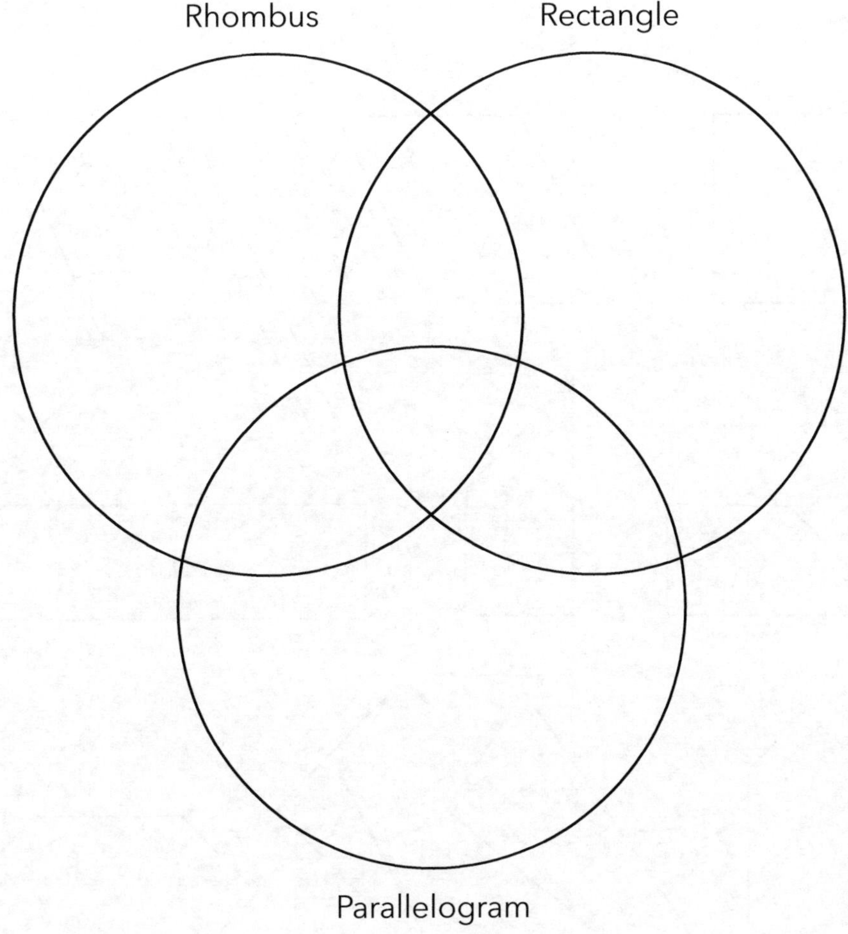

Extend Your Thinking

1. Create a Venn diagram and place the shapes in the correct places, but do not include the labels for the Venn diagram. Ask your partner to analyze the shapes in each section and determine the labels for each.

Geometry

NAME:______________________ DATE:__________

LESSON 5.1

Shapes

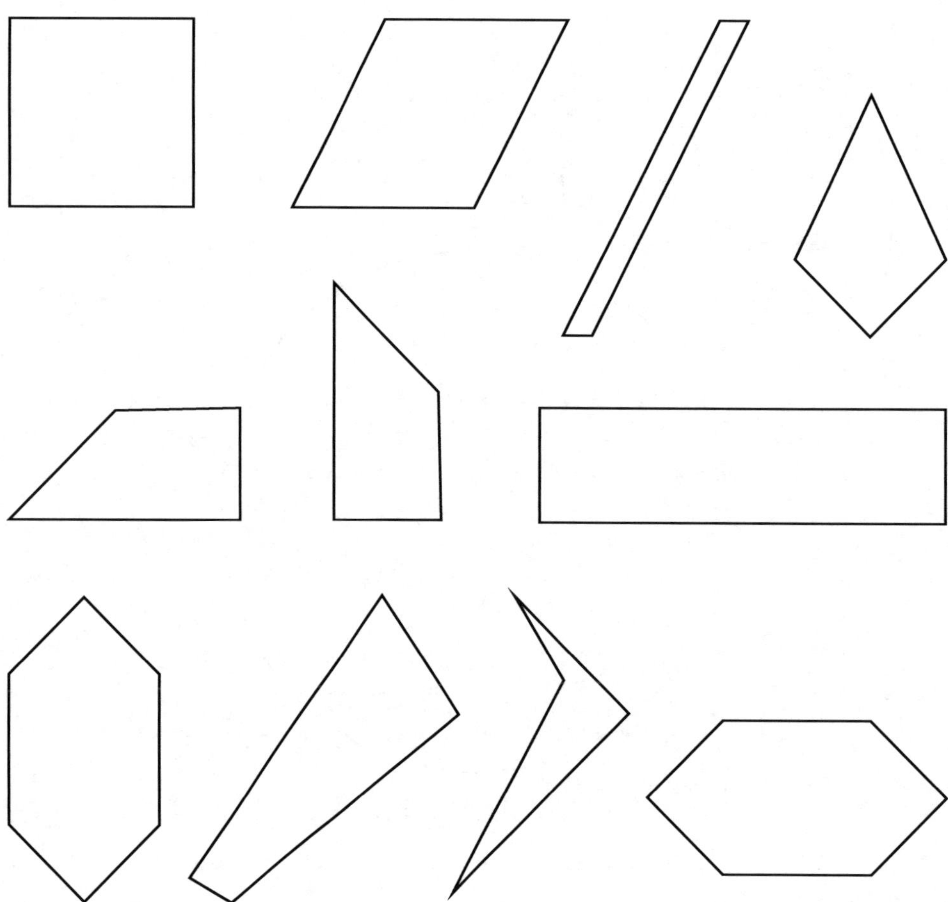

NAME:_______________________ DATE:_______________

LESSON 5.1 PRACTICE

Classifying Shapes

Directions: Complete the problems below.

1. This shape can be classified in several ways. Name five categories in which a square fits.

2. What is the broadest category that all of the shapes in this activity fit? All of the shapes we worked with today are __________________.

3. Draw a shape that is a quadrilateral but is not a rhombus, a rectangle, or a square.

4. Draw a rectangle and a square. Compare and contrast the two figures.

5. Describe the attributes of a trapezoid.

6. Study the placement of the shapes below. Decide on the label for each section of the Venn diagram. Write in the labels.

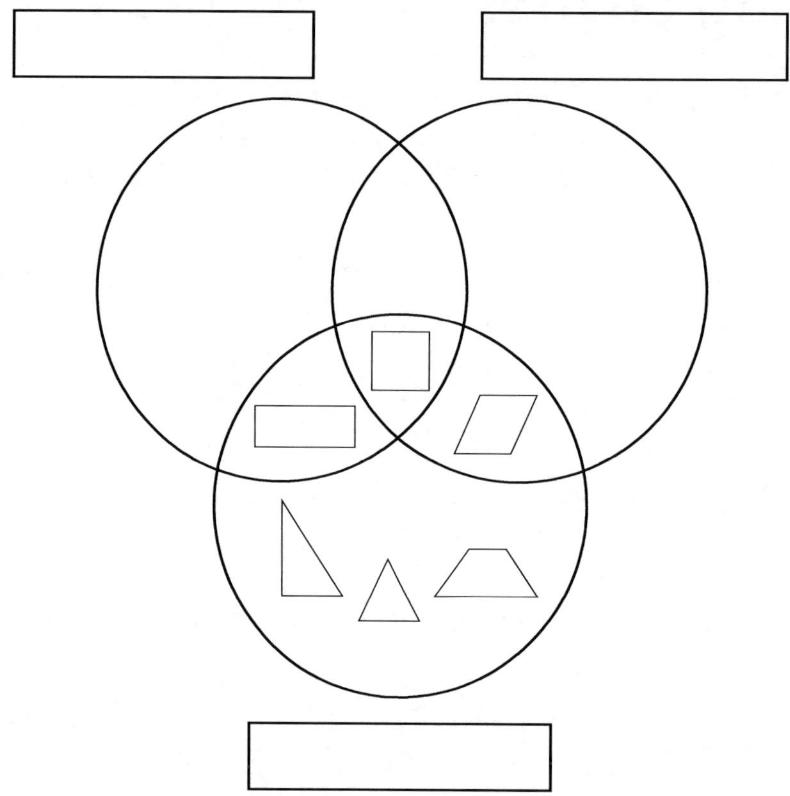

Extend Your Thinking

1. Create a tree model as a visual representation of the categories of shapes.

NAME:______________________________ DATE:______________

LESSON 5.1

Common Core Assessment Practice

Directions: Complete the problems below.

1. Rectangles and parallelograms have similar and unlike characteristics.
   a. Compare and contrast a rectangle and a parallelogram.

   b. Draw two figures that demonstrate the difference between the two terms.

2. Which shape is a rhombus?

   a. 

   b. 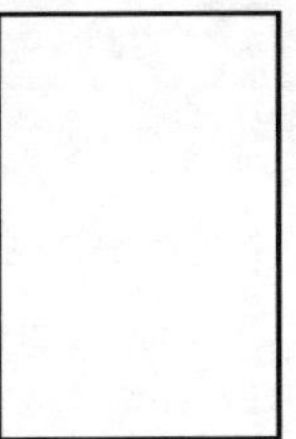

   c. 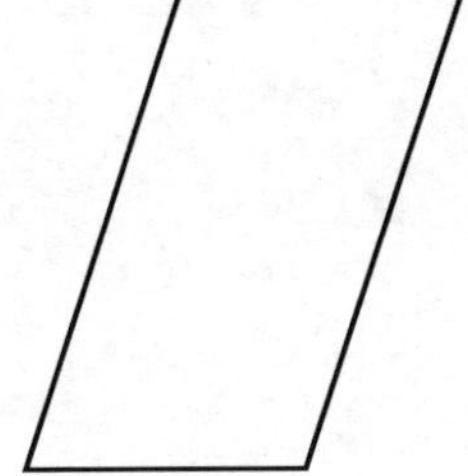

   d.

3. Classify the shape. Be as specific as you can.

4. Why isn't the shape in Number 3 a parallelogram? After explaining, extend lines on the picture to show why it isn't a parallelogram.

LESSON 5.2

Partition Shapes Into Equal Areas

Common Core State Standards

- 3.G.2

Mathematical Practices

- 2, 4, and 5

Estimated Time

- 60 minutes

Key Terms

- Partition

Materials

- Lesson 5.2 Activity: Partitioning
- Lesson 5.2 Shape Cards
- Lesson 5.2 Practice: Partitioning Shapes
- Lesson 5.2 Common Core Assessment Practice

Objectives

In this lesson, students will:

- partition shapes into parts with equal areas, and
- express partitioned parts of shapes as fraction pieces related to the whole.

Lesson 5.2 Activity: Partitioning

Lesson 5.2 Shape Cards include tangram shapes with statements regarding their size in comparison to unknown shapes. Students will work in pairs and place all of the cards so each person can see them. Partner A will find and read the card with the triangle that is labeled "First Card": "My area is $\frac{1}{6}$ of whose area?" Partner B then locates that card. Once the card is located, Student B will explain why the triangle's area is $\frac{1}{6}$ of the area on the card. The students will discuss and make sure Partner B is correct. Partner B then reads what that card says, and Partner A will look for the card being described and explain why it matches. Cards can be used more than once. After completing the card game, students will use tangram shapes to fill in the chart about the relationship between the area of one shape to the area of another shape.

NAME:______________________________ DATE:______________

Geometry

LESSON 5.2 ACTIVITY

Partitioning

Directions: Different shapes have different areas, but their areas are still related to one another. You and your partner will search for the card with the triangle that is labeled "First Card." Whoever finds it first will be Partner A. Partner A will read the card aloud, and Partner B will look through the other cards to find the card being described. Discuss with each other to decide if you agree upon the card choice. Continue play with Partner B reading the chosen card and Partner A finding the referenced card. Remember to place the cards back because they can be used more than once.

Once the game is complete, use the tangram shapes to help you fill out the chart below. List the first shape, state how its area is related to the second shape, and then draw a picture to model the relationship.

Shape 1	Area Relationship	Shape 2	Picture

Extend Your Thinking

1. Use tangram shapes to create a story about partitioning the area of shapes.

NAME:______________________________ DATE:______________

LESSON 5.2

Shape Cards

First Card
Triangle
My area is $\frac{1}{6}$ of whose area?

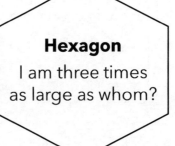

Hexagon

I am three times as large as whom?

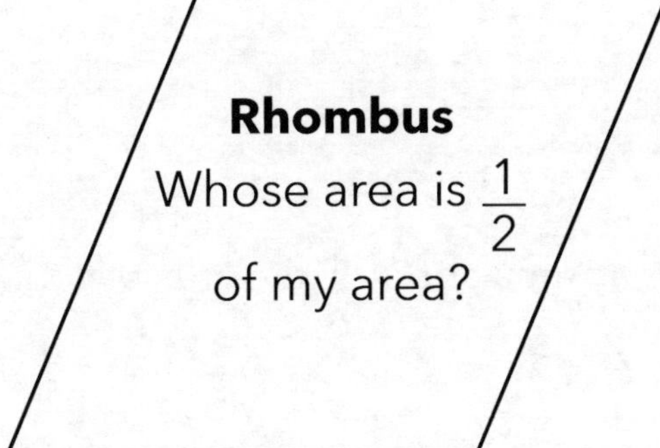
Rhombus
Whose area is $\frac{1}{2}$ of my area?

Square

My area is $\frac{1}{3}$ of whose area?

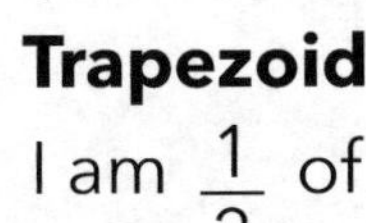
Trapezoid
I am $\frac{1}{2}$ of whose area?

NAME:________________________________ DATE:______________

LESSON 5.2 PRACTICE

Partitioning Shapes

Directions: Complete the problems below.

1. Consider the fractional pieces and draw the whole.

a. $\frac{1}{6}$

c. 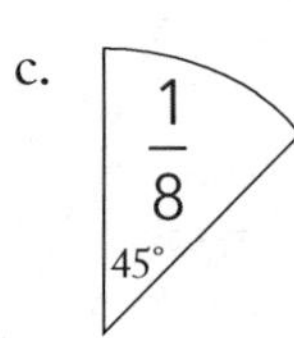

b. $\frac{1}{4}$

d. 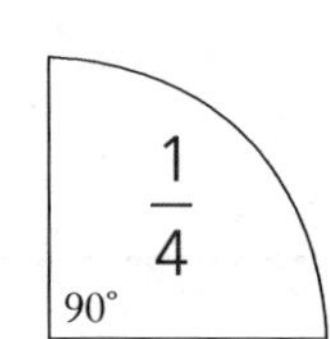

2. Name an item in your classroom that has an area about $\frac{1}{6}$ the area of your desktop.

____

3. Partition the following shapes to show the size of the fractional piece listed.

Shape	Fractional Piece	Drawing of Fractional Piece
	$\frac{3}{8}$	
	$\frac{1}{2}$	

Shape	Fractional Piece	Drawing of Fractional Piece
	$\frac{1}{4}$	Draw two different ways.
	$\frac{1}{4}$	Draw three different ways.

Extend Your Thinking

1. Trace the shapes in the table on Number 3 onto a clean sheet of paper. Partition each shape into a different number of sections.
   a. How many different ways are possible? ________
   b. Can each shape be broken into the same number of equal sections? ________

Geometry

LESSON 5.2

Common Core Assessment Practice

1. Draw a square and partition it into six parts. Shade three parts.

   a. What fraction of the shape is shaded? ________
   b. What fraction of the shape is not shaded? ________
   c. Why do the shaded and nonshaded portions on the shape have the same fraction?

2. For the shape to be partitioned into equal sections, estimate how many more lines need to be added.

   a. 8
   b. 2
   c. 7
   d. 3

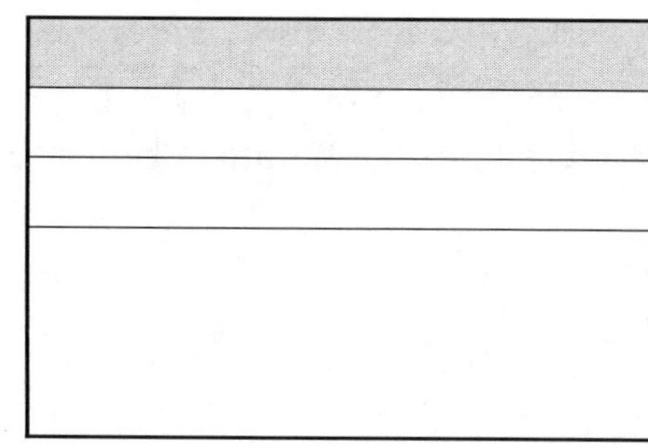

3. Samantha says that there is no need to add more lines to the above shape. Explain to Samantha why more lines must be added in order to determine what fractional amount has been shaded.

4. What fractional part has been shaded?

   a. $\frac{2}{3}$

   b. $\frac{5}{6}$

   c. $\frac{4}{4}$

   d. $\frac{4}{7}$

ANSWER KEY

SECTION I: NUMBER AND OPERATIONS IN BASE TEN

Lesson 1.1 Activity: Budget Plans for Businesses

1. Answers will vary.
2. Answers will vary.
3. \$450. Round each number to the nearest ten.
4. a. (\$43 + \$119) + \$58 = \$220; b. (\$58 + \$43) + \$119 = \$220; c. The two scenarios are equivalent due to the associative property of addition, which states that the grouping of addends in differing order doesn't affect the sum.
5. a. The partner rounded to the nearest hundred, and the student rounded to the nearest ten.

   b.

   Partner's Approach

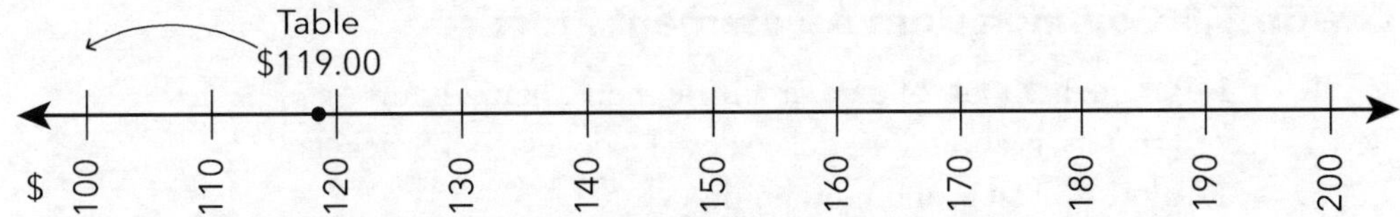

\$119.00 is closer to \$100.00 than \$200.00.
The partner rounded to the nearest hundred.

   c.

   Your Approach

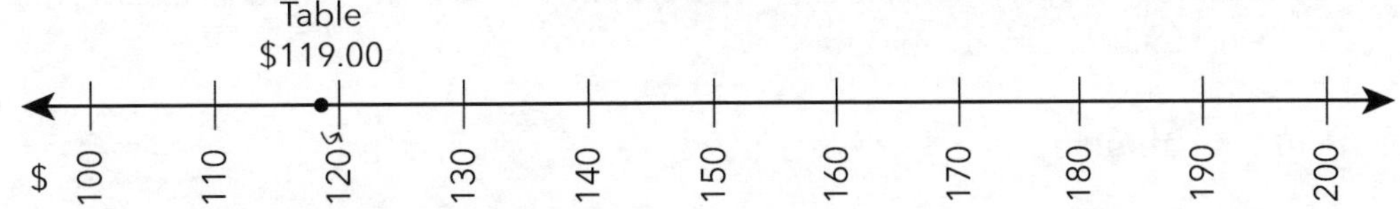

\$119.00 is closer to \$120.00 than \$110.00.
You rounded to the nearest ten.

Extend Your Thinking

1. Answers will vary.
2. Answers will vary.

Lesson 1.1 Practice: Place Value and Rounding

1. She should estimate. Eight bags are needed because $50 \times 8 = 400$. Seven bags would not be enough because $50 \times 7 = 350$.
2. Answers will vary.
3. Answers will vary.
4. 13
5. a. possible answers: $68 + 79 = 147$, $78 + 69 = 147$; b. possible answers: $98 + 76 = 174$, $78 + 96 = 174$; c. possible answers: $98 + 67 = 165$, $68 + 97 = 165$
6. The answer could also be either $76 + 89 = 165$ or $86 + 79 = 165$.
7. a. 325; b. 170
8. a. 4,194; b. 800
9. a. 385
10. a. about 2,700; b. about 170; c. 177

Extend Your Thinking

1. If the ones digit in the sum is 5, that means the ones digits of the addends have to add up to 5 or 15, 25, 35, etc. Looking at the given digits (6, 7, 8, 9), two sets of numbers add to 15: $8 + 7$ and $9 + 6$. Therefore, I know that 8 and 7 or 9 and 6 have to be in the ones place, leaving the other two numbers not selected for the tens place.
2. Answers will vary.

Lesson 1.1 Common Core Assessment Practice

1. a. 140 min.; b. about 2 hours or a little more than 2 hours
2. a. 258 tickets; b. about 340 tickets; c. 417 tickets; d. 78 tickets
3. a. 17 more points; b. about 60 points

Lesson 1.2 Activity: Mind Readers

1. Answers will vary. Possible answer: A multiple of 10 multiplied by a one-digit number is just like multiplying single-digit numbers and then placing a zero in the ones place as a place holder.
2. Answers will vary. Possible answer: The more factors that the products have, the more possible multiplication problems.

Extend Your Thinking

1. Answers will vary.
2. Answers will vary.

Lesson 1.2 Practice: Using Place Value

1. a. 80×7 or 70×8; b. No. It could be 80×7 or 70×8 (whichever one wasn't used already).
2. a. Both students are correct because 6 tens times $6 = 360$ and 9 tens times $4 = 360$. It shows that 360 has several factors. b. Answers will vary.
3. a. Both students are correct; b. Because 40 groups of 5 is equivalent to 5 groups of 40.
4. 15; tens; tens
5. Answers will vary. Students can use place value, grouping, or any other method to explain their answer.

Extend Your Thinking

1. Answers will vary.
2. Answers will vary.

Lesson 1.2 Common Core Assessment Practice

1. The product of 3 times 8 ones is 24 ones. The product of 3 times 8 tens is 24 tens, and the product of 8 times 3 tens is 24 tens. 24 tens is written as 240.
2. 120
3. 12; 12
4. A zero is added to show the place value. 70 represents 7 tens; therefore, the answer will be 35 tens, not 35 ones.
5. 200

SECTION II: OPERATIONS AND ALGEBRAIC THINKING

Activity 2.1: Proper Placement of Properties

Extend Your Thinking

1. Answers will vary.
2. Answers will vary.

Scenario Cards

1. Yes, I agree because $2(6 \times 7)$ can be read, "Two 6 x 7 arrays." Therefore, $(6 \times 7) + (6 \times 7) = 2(6 \times 7)$; to solve $2(6 \times 7)$, Sammy also could have made 7 different arrays, each representing the multiplication facts 2×6.
2. $(12 \times 10) + (12 \times 1)$; Answers will vary. Carolina could have broken the 11 into 5 and 6 because the sum of 5 and 6 is 11. The expression would be $(12 \times 5) + (12 \times 6)$.
3. $2 + 2$; $17 \times 4 = 17(2 + 2) = (17 \times 2) + (17 \times 2)$
4. 21; 21; Both Sue and her coach are correct. $21 \times 0 = 0 \times 21$ because of the commutative property of multiplication or the zero property of multiplication.
5. Each product equals the factor by which one is multiplied. The rule is the multiplicative property of one, which states that any factor times one will equal that factor.
6. Chastity knows that $(N \times 4)$ must equal 32, because the total (80) minus 8×6 (48) equals 32; $32 \div 4 = 8$, so $N = 8$.
7. 0; 1, as any number times 1 will equal the original number.
8. Answers will vary; Example: Using 10×6: 10 groups in the first array; 6 is the size of each group.
9. Yes, they will have the same product because of the zero property of multiplication. It doesn't matter if the size of the groups is zero or if the number of groups is zero, the product will be zero.
10. The products of the two multiplication problems that the student knows should be added together because $10 + 6 = 16$; therefore, $(5 \times 10) + (5 \times 6) = 5 \times 16$.
11. The commutative property of multiplication states that the order in which factors are multiplied doesn't affect the product, so $6 \times 3 = 18$ because $3 \times 6 = 18$.

12. $(7 \times 9) \times 8 = (8 \times 9) \times 7 = (7 \times 8) \times 9$; $(63) \times 8 = 504 = (72) \times 7 = 504 = (56) \times 9 = 504$
13. $56 + 98 = 154$
14. $(212 \times 10) + (212 \times 5)$ or $(200 \times 15) + (12 \times 15)$; No, these two strategies are not the only two ways to break up the numbers. Laverne can break 212 or 15 into any two addends that result in 212 or 15, as long as she can multiply efficiently by those numbers.

Lesson 2.1 Practice: Multiplication

1. a. $19 \times 8 = 152$; $8 \times 19 = 152$; b. $23 \times 7 = 161$; $7 \times 23 = 161$; The order that the factors are multiplied doesn't change the product; Answers will vary for student problems.
2. $7 \times 8 = 56$ and $2 \times 8 = 16$; $7 + 2 = 9$, so instead of 9×8, I can write $(7 + 2) \times 8 = (7 \times 8) + (2 \times 8) = 56 + 16 = 72 = 9 \times 8$
3. Answers will vary; a. Example: We have seven tables in our classroom. Each table has 12 books. How many books does our classroom have in all?; b. Example: Marquez had a bag of suckers split into groups of seven. He has 12 groups total. How many suckers did Marquez have?; c. The products are equal because of the commutative property of multiplication; Example: $12 \times 7 = 84$ and $7 \times 12 = 84$.
4. The associative property does not apply when you are subtracting.
5. Answers will vary; Example: $(6 \times 9) + (4 \times 9) = 54 + 36 = 90$ or (10×9); $(6 + 4) \times 9 = 10 \times 9 = 90$.

Extend Your Thinking

1. Answers will vary.

Lesson 2.1 Common Core Assessment Practice

1. b; Answers will vary.
2. a, b, c, d
3. d
4. b
5. c; The expression did not use the commutative property correctly. It added 13 and 5 to get 18 and then multiplied by 5.

Lesson 2.2 Activity: Multiply to Divide

Extend Your Thinking

1. Answers will vary; Example: 32 because the fact family could be $2 \times 16 = 32$, $16 \times 2 = 32$, $32 \div 16 = 2$, and $32 \div 2 = 16$ or $8 \times 4 = 32$, $4 \times 8 = 32$, $32 \div 8 = 4$, $32 \div 4 = 8$

Lesson 2.2 Practice: Division

1. 7:

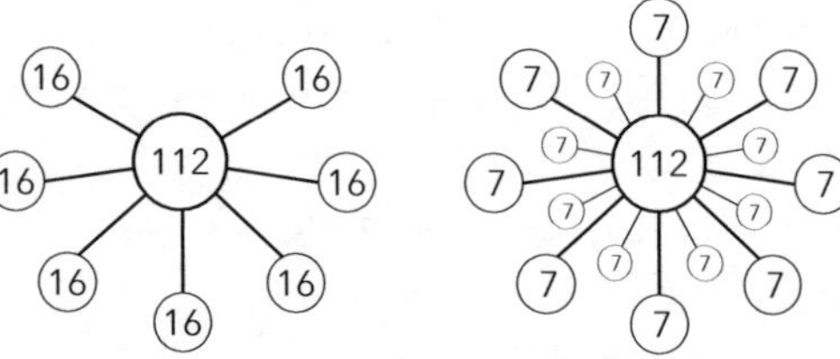

2. 2; 4; Fact families: 2, 16, 4, 8, 32
3. xxxxxx ; 9 × 6 = 54; The size of each group is 6.
   xxxxxx
   xxxxxx
   xxxxxx
   xxxxxx
   xxxxxx
   xxxxxx
   xxxxxx
   xxxxxx
4. a. 9; b. Answers will vary; Example: Students could divide 225 into 5 groups. Each group would have 45 Skittles. 5 × 45 = 225 Skittles; 225 ÷ 5 = 45 Skittles; c. Answers will vary; Example: 3 groups of 75 Skittles: 3 × 75 = 225; 225 ÷ 3 = 75; d. Because 225 doesn't divide by 26 evenly, students will need to decide what to do with the leftover candies (i.e., the remainders)—maybe they should go to the teacher!
5. 10 times; 110 ÷ 11 = 10
6. a. 7; 28 ÷ 7 = 4; b. 3; 36 ÷ 12 = 3; c. 3; 18 ÷ 6 = 3; d. Answers will vary. Examples: They are both multiples of 3; you can skip count by 3 and reach both numbers; they are both divisible by 3; 3 is a factor of both.

Lesson 2.2 Common Core Assessment Practice

1. 6; c; Expression A does not represent the problem because there are only 24 flowers total, not 24 groups of 4 flowers. Expression B does not represent the problem because there are only 4 arrangements with 24 total flowers, not 4 arrangements of 24 flowers each. Expression D would result in a number less than one. Expression C represents the problem because it is read as 24 flowers broken into 4 arrangements.
2. 7; b, c; Options B and C are expressions that can be used to solve the problem because they are inverse operations of each other. 3 × 7 = 21 and 21÷ 3 = 7
3. a; Option A is an expression that could help you solve 64 ÷ 8 because it is using the inverse operation. The expression represents, "8 × what number will give you 64?"
4. d:

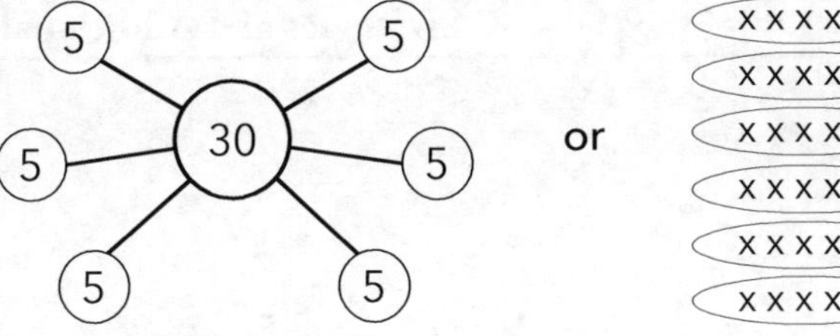

5 in each of the six groups

5 in each of the six groups

5. c; The equation in Option C is the inverse operation of 8 × P = 32. The unknown, P, is equal to 32 ÷ 8, which equals 4.
6. Both students are correct because 9 groups of 12 equals 108, and if 108 is divided into 2 groups, there will be 54 in each group. Both have a total of 108.

Lesson 2.3 Activity: Make the Match

1. Answers are in bold.

Equation 1	Equation 2	Property
$(11 \times 2) + (11 \times 10)$	11×12	**Distributive property**
$64 \div 8$	$8 \times n = 64$	**Inverse Operations**
25×7	$(20 + 5) \times 7$	**Distributive Property**
45×4	4×45	**Commutative Property**
$48 \div 6$	$(30 \div 6) + (18 \div 6)$	**Distributive Property**
$9 \times 6 \times 7$	$(9 \times 6)7$ or $(6 \times 7)9$ or $(7 \times 9)6$	**Associative Property**
$6(7 + 8)$	$(6 \times 7) + (6 \times 8)$	**Distributive Property**
$4 \times 3 \times 6$	$(4 \times 3)6$ or $(3 \times 6) \times 4$ or $(4 \times 6) \times 3$	**Associative Property**
$32 \div n = 8$	$8 \times n = 32$	**Inverse Operations**
$n \times 6 = 36$	$36 \div 6 = n$	**Inverse Operations**
$54 \div 6 = n$	$6 \times n = 54$	**Inverse Operations**
73×4	Multiply 73×2, and then double the product	**Strategies and Additional Problems**
79×10	$790 \div 2 = 79 \times 5$	**Strategies and Additional Problems**
37×9	$(37 \times 10) - (37 \times 1)$	**Strategies and Additional Problems**

Extend Your Thinking

1. Answers will vary.
2. $9 \times 25 = (10 \times 25) - (1 \times 25)$
   $9 \times 25 = (250) - (25)$
   $9 \times 25 = 225$

Lesson 2.3 Practice: Multiplication and Division

1. $16 \times 4 = (10 + 6)4 = (10 \times 4) + (6 \times 4) = 40 + 24 = 64$
2. $x = 40, p = 36, e = 56, n = 6$; If you double the product of a number times 4, it will result in that number times 8.
3. Mentally, 67×2 is easier to work with. $67 \times 2 = 134$. If you double that, you get $67 \times 4 = 268$. And if you double that, you get the product of $67 \times 8 = 536$.
4. a. 2; b. 2
5. Sedrick could add $7 \times 8 = 56$ to 320 to get the product of $47 \times 8 = 376$.

Lesson 2.3 Common Core Assessment Practice

1. b
2. a. 12; b. iii, iv; c. iii and iv can both be used to solve the expression because they are inverse operations of each other. 36 candles equals 12 candles in each box times 3 boxes. 36 candles broken into 3 boxes equals 12.
3. a
4. 28;

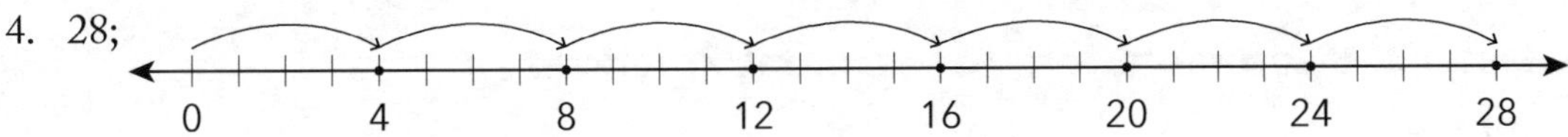

5. b

Lesson 2.4 Activity: Architect Arithmetic

Extend Your Thinking

1. Answers will vary.

The Leaning Tower of Pisa

1. a. 8 toothpicks representing 7 meters each. $56 \div n = 7$; b. The answer is reasonable because 56 broken into 8 groups equals 7.
2. The Leaning Tower of Pisa took 199 years to build; therefore, each time frame would be $33\frac{1}{3}$ years long.
3. 168 square meters
4. 6
5. 12
6. $33,015.48
7. $6,984.52

The Eiffel Tower

1. a. 300 meters $\div$ 20 meters = 15; b. The answer is reasonable because $20 \times 15 = 300$.
2. a. $300 \div 10 = N$, $N = 30$; b. $10 \times 30 = 300$
3. a. 3 breaks (555 steps each), 5 breaks (333 steps each), 9 breaks (185 steps each), 15 breaks (111 steps each), 37 breaks (45 steps each), 45 breaks (37 each); b. Answers will vary, but students should justify their work. For example: I would choose to take 15 breaks because I think building 111 steps before taking a break for a couple of days would be reasonable and will still get the job done quickly.
4. You need 335 more steps. $1,665 + 335 = 2,000$

The Statue of Liberty

1. Each toothpick will represent 18 meters. $5 \times N = 90$, $N = 18$; b. It is reasonable because $90 \div 5 = 18$.
2. a. $90 \div 2 = 45$; b. $45 \times 2 = 90$
3. a. 336 square feet; b. $336 \div 24 = 14$
4. a. Students must first solve $1,274 + $1,274, or $1,274 × 2, which equals $2,548. They then add $2,548 + $984.99 = $3532.99; b. $2,548.00 – $984.99 = $1,563.01

The Great Pyramid

1. a. You will need 10 toothpicks. $45 \times N = 450, N = 10$; b. It is reasonable because $450 \div 45 = 10$.
2. a. $450 \div 5 = N, N = 90$; b. $90 \times 5 = 450$
3. a. 305 feet wider; b. It is reasonable because $755 - 450 = 305$.
4. a. $190 \div 5 = 38$ and $38 \times 75 = \$2,850$; b. $3 \times \$150 = \$450$ and $\$2,850 - \$450 = \$2,400$

Lesson 2.4 Common Core Assessment Practice

1. c
2. c
3. b
4. $2 \times b = 74; b = 37$
5. Division can be used because multiplication and division are inverse operations. You can divide to solve, but you can also ask yourself, two times what number would equal 74? $37 \times 2 = 74$. The division problem would say $74 \div 2 = 37$.

Lesson 2.5 Activity: Chef's Choice

Meal Request Cards

1 meat: ham 1 vegetable: broccoli 1 sweet: chocolate pie Meat: 2,208 calories Vegetable: 150 calories Sweet: 903 calories	2 meats: turkey, steak 1 fruit: cantaloupe 1 vegetable: cauliflower 2 carbohydrates: baked potato, rice 1 sweet: pecan pie Meat: 4,460 calories Fruit: 300 calories Vegetable: 730 calories Carbohydrates: 1,725 calories Sweet: 585 calories
2 servings of chicken 1 fruit: strawberries 1 vegetable: sweet potato 2,754 calories	1 serving of spaghetti 1 carbohydrate: roll 1 sweet: chocolate pie Tomato

Extend Your Thinking

1. Answers will vary.
2. Answers will vary.

Lesson 2.5 Practice: Multistep Word Problems

1. a. $140 \div 20 = 7, 7 \times 4 = 28$; b. $20 - 4 = 16, 16 \times 7 = 112$; c. $112 - 28 = 84$
2. a. $150 \div 25 = 6$; b. 12 chips at 6 calories each equals 72 calories. Eating 13 chips would be too many because $13 \times 6 = 78$. So, you can eat 12 chips, and you started with 25, $25 - c = 12; c = 13$. You need to give away 13 chips. The answer is reasonable because the 12 chips eaten and the 13 chips given away add up to 25 chips total.

3. a. 2 friends because $160 \div 2 = 80$ calories each, 4 friends because $160 \div 4 = 40$ calories each, 5 friends because $160 \div 5 = 32$ calories each, 8 friends because $160 \div 8 = 20$ calories each, 10 friends because $160 \div 10 = 16$ calories each; b. Each chip has 8 calories because $160 \div 20 = 8$. 5 chips should be given away because 20 chips − 5 chips = 15 chips. 15 chips × 8 calories each = 120 calories.

Extend Your Thinking

1. Answers will vary.
2. Answers will vary.

Lesson 2.5 Common Core Assessment Practice

1. 144
2. 148
3. 36
4. $4
5. $60

Lesson 2.6 Activity: What's the Pattern?

Chart 1

1. It equals an odd number.
2. Answers will vary.

Chart 2

1. a. It equals an even number; b. It equals an odd number.
2. Answers will vary.

Chart 3

1. a. It is skip counting by 4; b. It equals an even number.
2. I do agree with Tony, because the product of a number times 4 is double the product of that same number times 2. The product of a number times 2 is half the product of that same number times 4. For example, $14 \times 2 = 28$ and $14 \times 4 = 56$. 28 doubled equals 56 and half of 56 equals 28.

Extend Your Thinking

1. Answers will vary.
2. Answers will vary.

Lesson 2.6 Practice: Patterns

1. Students should highlight a row and column supporting the commutative property of multiplication.
2. a. Even products; b. Even products; c. Odd products
3. An even number plus an even number equals an even number (such as $28 + 18 = 46$). An odd number plus an odd number equals an even number such as ($21 + 9 = 30$). An even number plus an odd number equals an odd number (such as $24 + 13 = 37$).

Extend Your Thinking

1. Answers will vary.

Lesson 2.6 Common Core Assessment Practice

1. Answers will vary. Possible answer: 7; 49; 343; 2,401
2. d
3. a
4. Answers are in bold.

Lawns Mowed	Money
1	$19.00
2	$26.00
3	**$33.00**
4	**$40.00**
5	$47.00
6	**$54.00**

SECTION III: NUMBER AND OPERATIONS—FRACTIONS

Lesson 3.1 Activity: Fractional Lengths

1. a. 2; b. 4 in.
2. a. 4; b. 2 in.
3. a. 5; b. Approximately $1\frac{1}{2}$ in. ($\approx 1\frac{2}{3}$ in.)
4. a. 6; b. Approximately $1\frac{1}{4}$ in. ($\approx 1\frac{1}{3}$ in.)
5. a. 8; b. 1 in.
6. a. 10; b. Approximately $\frac{3}{4}$ in.
7. a. 12; b. Approximately $\frac{1}{2}$ in. ($\approx \frac{2}{3}$ in.)

Extend Your Thinking

1. You would need to have two whole straws (pipes) and then you would cut another whole straw into thirds. Each section would be $2\frac{2}{3}$ inches. $2\frac{1}{3}$ would be represented with the 2 whole pipes and $\frac{1}{3}$ of the pipe that was cut.

Lesson 3.1 Practice

1. a. $\frac{3}{18}$ or $\frac{1}{6}$; b. $\frac{15}{18}$ or $\frac{5}{6}$
2. a. $\frac{6}{18}$ or $\frac{1}{3}$; b. $\frac{12}{18}$ or $\frac{2}{3}$

3. Thursday night's movie got better attendance because 15 out of the 18 people stayed, while only 12 of the 18 people stayed on Friday.

4. a. $\frac{4}{8}$ or $\frac{1}{2}$; b. $\frac{2}{8}$ or $\frac{1}{4}$

   c. Pepperoni sold more pieces:

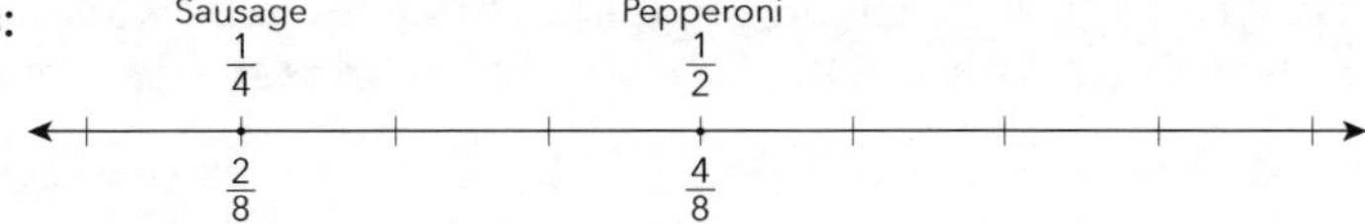

5. Jeremiah is correct because even though he and Kerri both ate the whole pizza, the wholes were different sizes and it isn't an equal comparison.

Extend Your Thinking

1. Answers will vary.

Lesson 3.1 Common Core Assessment Practice

1.

2.

3. d

4.

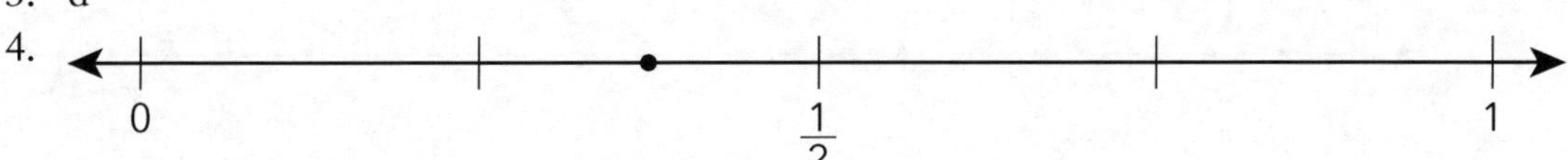

Answers will vary.

5.

0 1/2 1

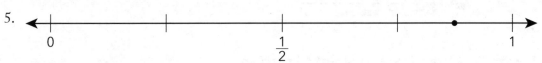

Answers will vary.

Lesson 3.2 Activity: Equivalence

Only answers are shown.

Given Fraction	Equivalent Fraction Card	Equivalent Fraction Card	Create Equivalent Fraction
			$\frac{6}{24}$
		$\frac{2}{3}$	30; the fraction would be $\frac{20}{30}$
			6
	$\frac{1}{2}$	$\frac{25}{50}$	14

Extend Your Thinking

1. Answers will vary.
2.

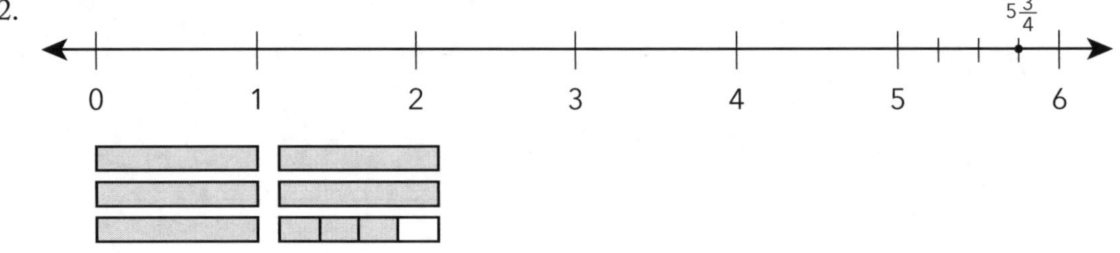

Lesson 3.2 Practice: Equivalent Fractions

1. a. Ian and Carlie both have the same size of cake (whole), but Carlie just cut hers into smaller pieces. Her cake wasn't bigger than Ian's.
   b. Cut Ian's first two rows of cake into thirds:

   Ian

2. a. $\frac{9}{9}$; b. 1 whole

3. $\frac{90}{9}$; there are 90 total slices in all 10 pizzas and each pizza is cut into 9 slices; therefore, 90 slices total divided by 9 slices each equals 10 whole pizzas.

Extend Your Thinking

1. When multiplying a numerator and a denominator by the same number, the number of parts increases and the size of the parts decrease. For example, take the fraction $\frac{1}{4}$. Create an equivalent fraction by multiplying the numerator and the denominator by 2. The answer will be $\frac{2}{8}$. Each of the four sections got two times smaller and the shape is now broken into 8 total parts.

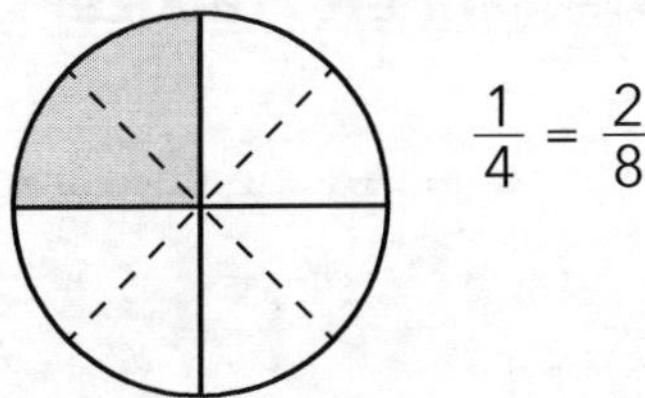

Lesson 3.2 Common Core Assessment Practice

1. b
2. $\frac{6}{8}$ is equivalent to $\frac{3}{4}$ because if you have two objects of the same size and break one into 8 parts and shade 6 parts and break the other object into 4 parts and shade 3, you will have the same amount shaded. $3 \times 2 = 6$ and $4 \times 2 = 8$
3. $\frac{4}{6}$ or $\frac{2}{3}$
4. No, because even though the fractions match, they aren't referring to the same whole and are not the same measurement.
5. Answers will vary. Students can draw two groups of 21 for a grand total of 42. Students might draw an array and cut it in half.

Lesson 3.3 Activity: Comparing Fractions

Extend Your Thinking

1. Answers will vary.

Comparing Fractions Chart

1. Answers will vary.
2. Answers will vary.
3. Answers will vary.

Lesson 3.3 Practice: Comparing Fractions

1. Marvin really ate more because his pie was cut into five pieces, which would be larger slices than Peter's pie. Peter's seven slices are smaller, so eating one slice is still eating less than

Marvin. Student's pictures should show two wholes the same size, one sliced into 5 sections, and the other 7. The shaded portion on the $\frac{1}{5}$ pie should be larger.

2. Even though both classes had $\frac{1}{2}$ the students score high enough for the A honor roll, half of 20 is less than half of 26. Therefore, more students made A honor roll in Mrs. Haynes's class.
3. When comparing fractions with common denominators, the fraction with the larger numerator is the larger fraction.
4. If the fractions are not referring to the same whole but have the same numerators, the fraction with the smaller denominator is the larger fraction.

Lesson 3.3 Common Core Assessment Practice

1. b
2. The drama movies represent the larger fraction because she rented 4 out of 5 versus 4 out of 7.
3. d
4. a

SECTION IV: MEASUREMENT AND DATA

Lesson 4.1 Activity: Scheduling

Answers will vary; Possible answer:

Reading	8:05–9:35	90 min.
Physical Education	9:35–10:05	30 min.
Math	10:05–11:35	90 min.
Recess	11:35–11:50	15 min.
Lunch	11:50–12:12	22 min.
Science	12:12–12:47	35 min.
Break	12:47–1:02	15 min.
Social Studies	1:02–1:32	30 min
Break	1:32–1:47	15 min.
Language	1:47–2:14	27 min.
Music	2:14–2:41	27 min.

Extend Your Thinking

1. Answers will vary.

Lesson 4.1 Practice

1. 42 minutes; b. 28 minutes; c. 2 hours and 40 minutes; d. 18 minutes short
2. a. 11:25 a.m.; b. Answers will vary, but students should show their work; c. 11:50 a.m.; d. 12:20 p.m.; e. 80 minutes, or 1 hour 20 minutes

3. Answers will vary based on the time of day; a. 5:45 p.m.; b. Students' clocks should show an hour hand almost to 8 and the correct minute hand should be drawn.

Extend Your Thinking

1. Students' clocks should show the following times:
   Leave work: 11:25
   Get to café: 11:50
   Finish eating: 12:20

Lesson 4.1 Common Core Assessment Practice

1. Clock should read 7:57.
2. Students should draw a number line to show their work. The start time is 5:18.
3. a
4. d

Lesson 4.2 Activity: Volume and Mass

Volume Part I

1. Answers will vary.
2. a. 10; b. 100 ml × 10 = n; c. 1,000 ml

Volume Part II

1. Answers will vary.
2. Answers will vary.

Mass Part I

1. Answers will vary.
2. Answers will vary.
3. Answers will vary.

Mass Part II

1. 10; a. 100 g × 10 = n; b. 1,000

Extend Your Thinking

1. Answers will vary.
2. Answers will vary.

Lesson 4.2 Practice: Volume and Mass

1. a. 9 liters; b. 100
2. a. 23 kg × 2 shoes per child = 46 kg; b. 75 kg – 46 kg = 29 kg; 29 shoes are needed. Therefore, 15 kids are needed because 15 kids × 2 shoes equals 30. One shoe will not be used.
3. 189 ÷ 7 = 27
4. a. 9; b. The mass of each item must be less than 1 kilogram.
5. a. 2 kg and 675 g; b. 325 g

Lesson 4.2 Common Core Assessment Practice

1. c
2. b
3. b
4. 168; $6 \times 7 \times 4 = 168$
5. 37 g

Lesson 4.3 Activity: Let's Graph It

1. Answers will vary.
2. a. Answers will vary; b. Answers will vary.
3. Answers will vary.
4. Answers will vary.
5. Answers will vary.

Extend Your Thinking

1. Answers will vary.

Lesson 4.3 Practice: Scaled Graphs

1. a. 16; b. Left handed because 16 total students were asked, and 4 students are left handed. $\frac{1}{4}$ of 16 is 4; c. 8; d. 3
2. a. Answers will vary; b. 3 because all of the numbers are multiples of 3 except one number; c. 5; d. 34; e. Classical

Lesson 4.3 Common Core Assessment Practice

1. b
2. a. 3; b. 33; c. 9
3. 

Lesson 4.4 Activity: Length of Our Limbs

1. Answers will vary.
2. Answers will vary.
3. Answers will vary.
4. Answers will vary.
5. Answers will vary.

Extend Your Thinking

1. Answers will vary.

Lesson 4.4 Practice: Measurement Data

1. a.11; b. 8 more marbles rolled more than 3 inches than less than 3 inches.
2. a. 10 or $\frac{10}{4}$; b. 2; c. $\frac{2}{4}$ or $\frac{1}{2}$; d. $\frac{2}{4}$ of an inch

Extend Your Thinking

1. Answers will vary.

Lesson 4.4 Common Core Assessment Practice

1. a
2. $3\frac{3}{4}$ inch
3. c
4. I would need to trim $\frac{6}{4}$. One whole inch and $\frac{1}{2}$ of another inch.

Lesson 4.5 Activity: Floor Plans

1. a. Figure A: 45 sq. cm; b. Figure B: 16 sq. cm; c. Figure C: 56 sq. cm
2. Answers will vary.
3. The factors of 15 are 1, 3, 5, and 15, so all of the rectangular-shaped rooms have been created; a. Answers will vary, but should mention the factors of 15; b. The order in which factors are multiplied does not affect the product (commutative property of multiplication).
4. 1 x 18, 18 x 1, 2 x 9, 9 x 2, 3 x 6, 6 x 3; a. Answers will vary; Hallways are usually connecting rooms so they are often long and narrow (1 x 18).
5. 1 x 32, 32 x 1, 2 x 16, 16 x 2, 4 x 8, 8 x 4; a. Answers will vary.

Extend Your Thinking

1. Answers will vary.

Lesson 4.5 Practice: Area

1. Figure 1: Students should have measured 8 cm x 8 cm for an area of 64 square centimeters. Figure 2: Students should have measured 17 cm x 5 cm for an area of 85 square centimeters. Students can use rulers, count the squares using the transparent paper, or any effective method that they choose.
2. 1 x 24, 24 x 1, 2 x 12, 12 x 2, 3 x 8, 8 x 3, 4 x 6, 6 x 4
3. 1, 22, 11, 2
4. The area inside a figure can be long and narrow or shorter and wider, but the amount of space inside the figures is the same.
5. Divide the figure into smaller segments that do represent a rectangle and then multiply the length and width of each section. Add the area of each section to get the area of the entire shape.

Extend Your Thinking

1. Answers will vary.

Lesson 4.5 Common Core Assessment Practice

1. c
2. a
3. Answers will vary but responses must represent knowledge of area.

Lesson 4.6 Activity: Area and Multiplication

1. Students should place the rectangles in order from least to greatest based on their estimate.
2. Answers will vary.
3. Students should ensure that the rectangles are placed in the correct order (1 x 6, 4 x 2, 8 x 4, 3 x 11, 8 x 5, 11 x 4).

Extend Your Thinking

1. Answers will vary.

Lesson 4.6 Practice: Area and Multiplication

1. a. 10 x 13 because there are 10 total rows and 13 columns. If you multiply 10×13, you will get the area (130). b. $5 \times 13 = 45$
2. a. 1 x 72, 72 x 1, 2 x 36, 36 x 2, 6 x 12, 12 x 6, 8 x 9, 9 x 8; b. 72; c. 1
3. a. 16; b. $16 + 16 + 16 + 16$; c. $4 \times 16 = 64$
4. 78 square feet
5. $98 more
6. Answers will vary but multiplication is the most efficient because it is less time consuming and the other options are getting the same answer by breaking down multiplication.

Lesson 4.6 Common Core Assessment Practice

1. a
2. c
3. $2 \times 3 = 6$; There are two rows and three in each row.
4. Answers will vary; Students might draw a 3 x 2 array because of the commutative property of multiplication.

Lesson 4.7 Activity: Area and Addition

1. a.

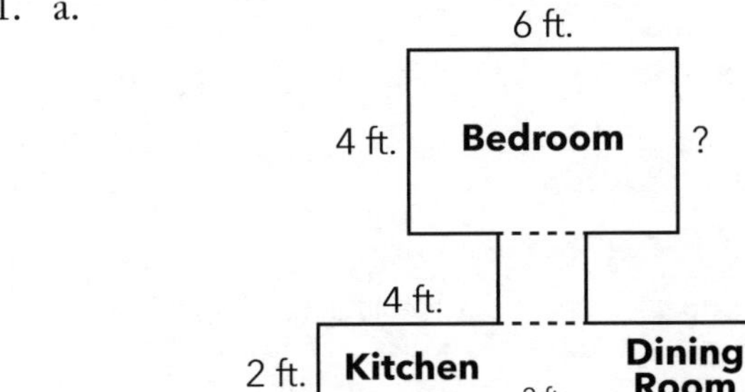

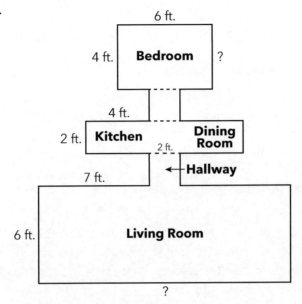

Note. For question a, the kitchen and dining room labels may be interchanged by your students.

b. 148 square feet

2. a.

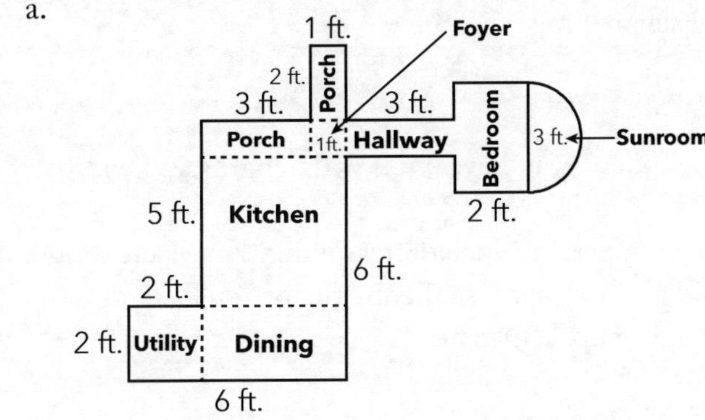

b. 45.5 square feet

3. a.

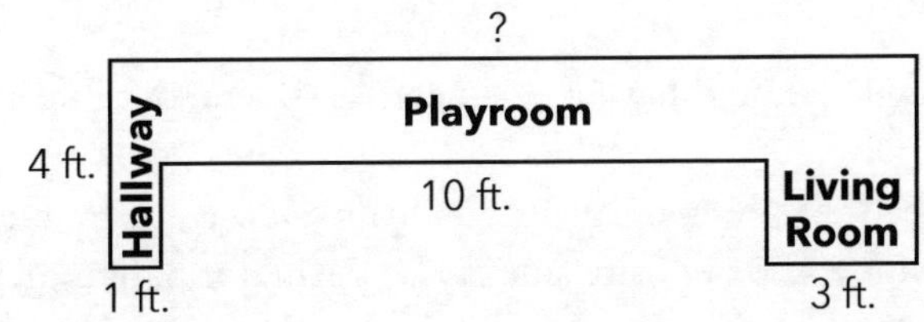

b. 36 square feet

Lesson 4.7 Practice: Area and Addition

1. 28 square feet
2. $14 \times 4 = 56$

3. $14 \times 10 = 140$
4. $(14 \times 4) + (14 \times 10) = 56 + 140 = 196$; $14 \times 14 = 196$
5. Answers will vary.
6. Answers will vary; Possible answer: $(16 \times 5) + (16 \times 1) = 80 + 16 = 96$; $16 \times 6 = 96$

Lesson 4.7 Common Core Assessment Practice

1. 14 centimeters squared
2. a. $4 \times 1 = 4$ and $2 \times 5 = 10$ or $6 \times 1 = 6$ and $2 \times 4 = 8$; b. $(4 \times 1) + (2 \times 5) = 14$
3. c
4. a. Answers will vary; b. Answers will vary.

Lesson 4.8 Activity: Polygon Perimeter

1. a. Answers will vary, but include 1 x 100, 100 x 1, 2 x 50, 50 x 2, 25 x 4, 4 x 25, 20 x 5, 5 x 20, 10 x 10; b. Answers will vary, but include 50 x 2, 2 x 50, 20 x 5, 5 x 20, 10 x 10, 4 x 25, 25 x 4); c. The pool with the largest perimeter would not be the best option for the family who likes to swim and play because it will be a long, skinny pool with not much room to play. This pool would be a better lap swimming pool.
2. a. The area of the pools would not be the same. The longer the length and shorter the width, the more the area increases; b. 1 x 23, 2 x 22, 3 x 21, 4 x 20, 5 x 19, 1.5 x 22.5, 2.5 x 21.5, 3.5 x 20.5); c. Answers will vary.
3. a. Width = 16 ft. The area is 128 square feet; b. . . . the area gets larger; c. This is not always true. It is only true until the length and width are equal. If the length and width were both 12, the area still got larger (144 square units); d. 23 feet

Extend Your Thinking

1. Answers will vary. For example, students can have pools with lengths and widths of 13 x 5, 15 x 3, etc.
2. Justifications will vary, but students need to include reasoning. For example, the circular pool would be best for swimming lessons because the instructor could stand in the middle and monitor while everyone is in reachable distance.

Lesson 4.8 Practice: Perimeter of Polygons

1. 12 cm
2. 3 in., 36 in., 3 in., 36 in.
3. 108 square inches
4. Answers will vary. Both rectangles should have a perimeter of 52 cm, but one should have a different area than the other.
5. A rectangle has opposite sides that are congruent. So if one side is 71 in. and the total perimeter is 148 in., then we know the opposite side is also 71 in. for a total of 142 inches. We still need 6 inches divided by two sides, so each side is 3 inches.

Lesson 4.8 Common Core Assessment Practice

1. b

2. The two models both have an area of 24 square yards, but the perimeter of the figures are different, and therefore their shape is different:

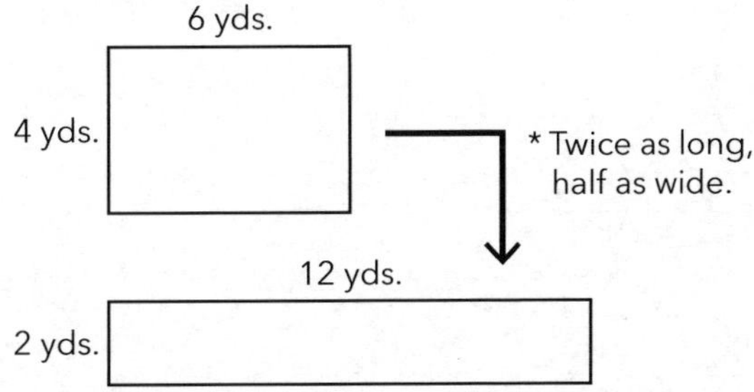

3. d
4. b

SECTION V: GEOMETRY

Lesson 5.1 Activity: Classifying Shapes

1.

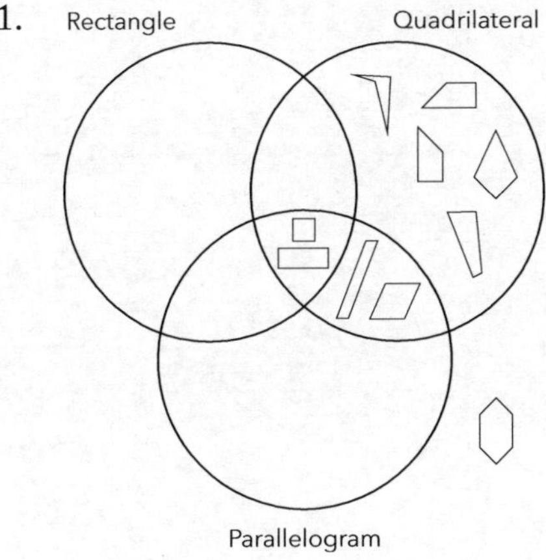

2. All parallelograms are quadrilaterals.

3.

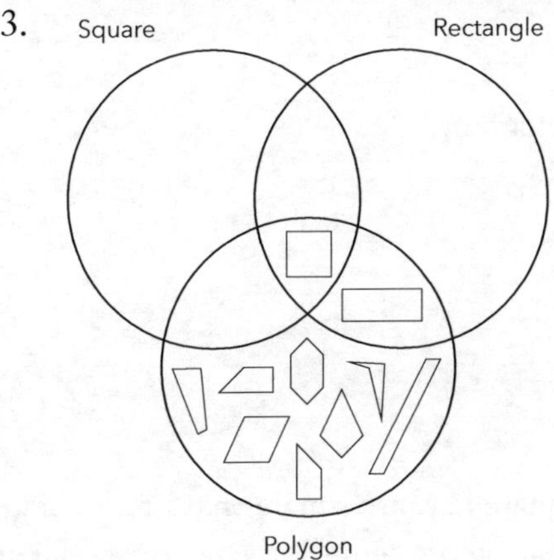

4. Square

5.

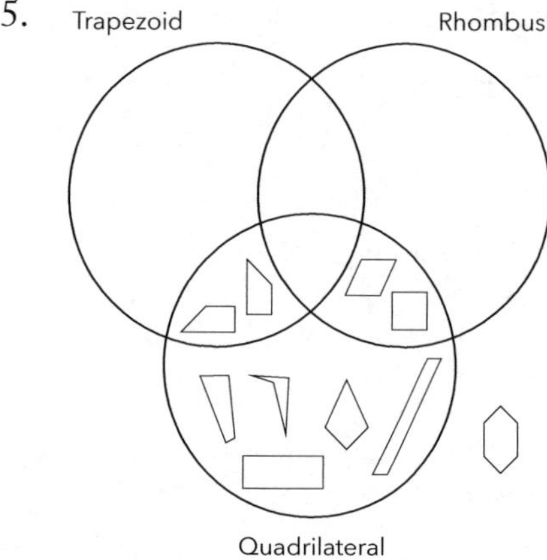

6. A trapezoid is a quadrilateral, but not a parallelogram because it only has one set of parallel sides. A rhombus is a quadrilateral and a parallelogram with four congruent sides. Therefore, a trapezoid cannot be a rhombus. A quadrilateral is a polygon with four sides.

7.

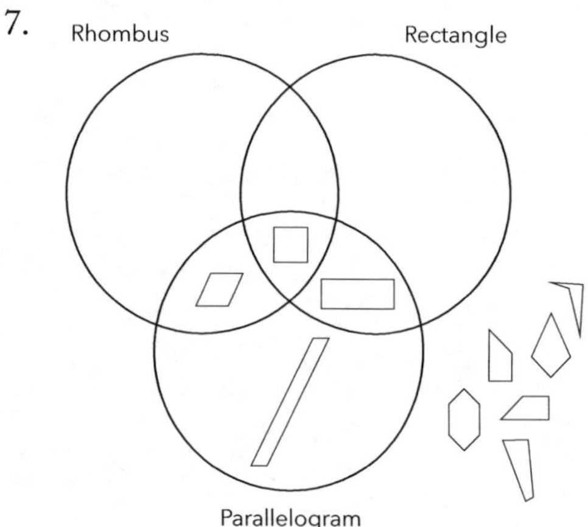

Extend Your Thinking

1. Answers will vary.

Lesson 5.1 Practice: Classifying Shapes

1. Rhombus, quadrilateral, square, rectangle, parallelogram
2. Polygons
3.

4. A square is a rectangle but a rectangle is not a square because squares have four congruent sides whereas rectangles have opposite sides that are congruent. Both shapes are quadrilaterals and have four right angles. Both shapes are also parallelograms.
5. A trapezoid is a polygon that is four-sided (quadrilateral) with one pair of parallel sides.

6. The top left should be labeled Rectangle, the top right should be labeled Rhombus, and the bottom section should be labeled Polygons.

Extend Your Thinking

1. Answers will vary.

Lesson 5.1 Common Core Assessment Practice

1. a. A rectangle has four right angles, and opposite sides that are congruent. A parallelogram has two pairs of parallel sides;

   b.

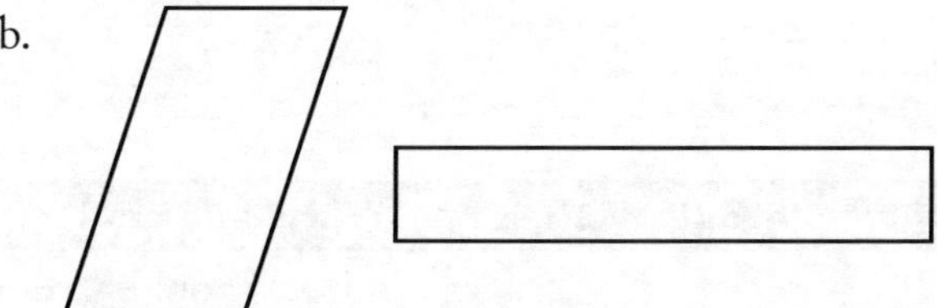

2. a
3. Polygon, trapezoid, quadrilateral
4. Parallelograms have two pairs of opposite sides that are parallel. Students should extend the left and right ends to show where they would eventually intersect.

Lesson 5.2 Activity: Partitioning

Order in table will vary, but students should include these answers.

- Triangle: My area is $\frac{1}{6}$ of whose area? Hexagon
- Hexagon: I am three times as large as whom? Rhombus
- Rhombus: Whose area is $\frac{1}{2}$ of my area? Triangle
- Square: My area is $\frac{1}{3}$ of whose area? Trapezoid
- Trapezoid: I am $\frac{1}{2}$ of whose area? Hexagon

Extend Your Thinking

1. Answers will vary.

Lesson 5.2 Practice: Partitioning Shapes

1. a.

   b.

c.

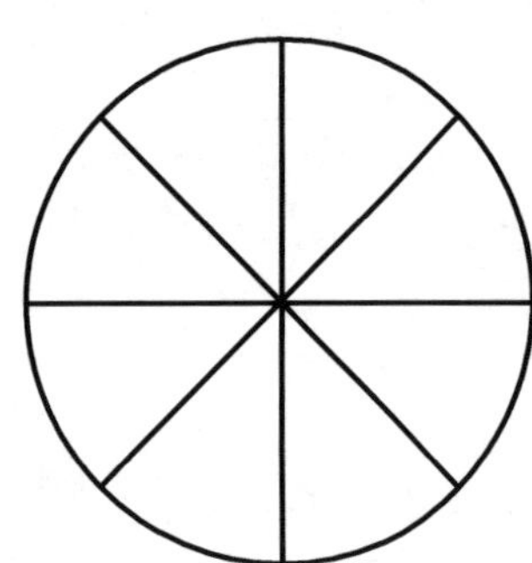

d.

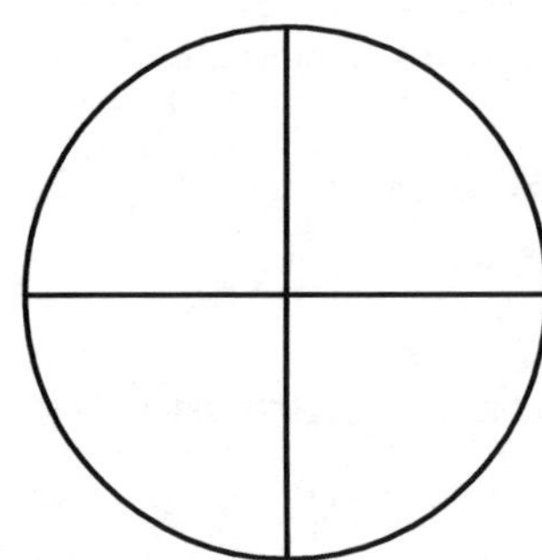

2. Answers will vary. Example: Notebook
3.

Shape	Fractional Piece	Drawing of Fractional Piece
	$\frac{3}{8}$	Students should partition shape to show $\frac{3}{8}$.
	$\frac{1}{2}$	Students should partition shape to show $\frac{1}{2}$.
	$\frac{1}{4}$	Students should partition shape to show $\frac{1}{4}$ in two different ways.
	$\frac{1}{4}$	Students should partition shape to show $\frac{1}{4}$ in three different ways.

Extend Your Thinking

1. a. The possibilities are endless as long as the partitioned segments are equivalent to each other:

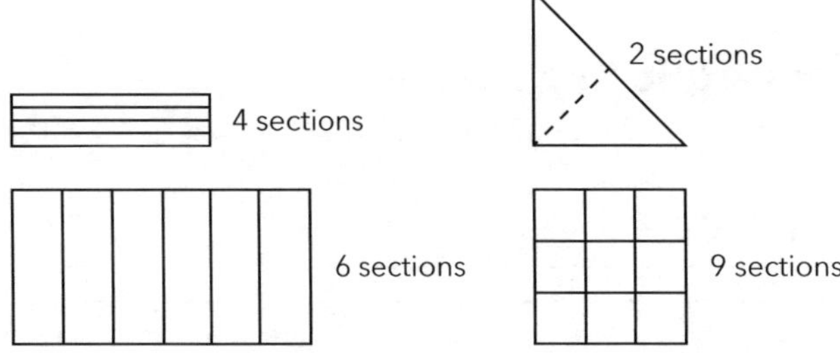

   b. The only way the shapes can all be broken into equal sections is if they are partitioned into two parts, because the triangle is not a quadrilateral and therefore does not have near as many lines of symmetry.

Lesson 5.2 Common Core Assessment Practice

1. a. $\frac{3}{6}$ or $\frac{1}{2}$; b. $\frac{3}{6}$ or $\frac{1}{2}$; c. They have the same fraction because the total shape was partitioned into 6 parts and 3 is half of 6, so 3 parts plus 3 parts will equal 6 total parts. $\frac{3}{6} = \frac{1}{2}$
2. b
3. In order to determine a fractional amount, the shape must be partitioned into equal sections.
4. a

ABOUT THE AUTHOR

Margaret Jess McKowen Patti is currently a third- and fourth-grade special education teacher of gifted students at Zachary Elementary School in Louisiana, where she recently received the Zachary Community School District Teacher of the Year award. Formerly, Jess taught second and fifth grade. She attended Southeastern Louisiana University, where she earned her bachelor's degree in elementary education, grades first through fifth. Jess then returned to Southeastern Louisiana University, where she obtained her master's degree in special education: gifted.

COMMON CORE STATE STANDARDS ALIGNMENT

Lesson	Common Core State Standards
Lesson 1.1	3.NBT.A Use place value understanding and properties of operations to perform multi-digit arithmetic.
Lesson 1.2	3.NBT.A Use place value understanding and properties of operations to perform multi-digit arithmetic.
Lesson 2.1	3.OA.A Represent and solve problems involving multiplication and division. 3.OA.B Understand properties of multiplication and the relationship between multiplication and division.
Lesson 2.2	3.OA.A Represent and solve problems involving multiplication and division. 3.OA.B Understand properties of multiplication and the relationship between multiplication and division.
Lesson 2.3	3.OA.A Represent and solve problems involving multiplication and division. 3.OA.B Understand properties of multiplication and the relationship between multiplication and division. 3.OA.C Multiply and divide within 100.
Lesson 2.4	3.OA.A Represent and solve problems involving multiplication and division.
Lesson 2.5	3.OA.D Solve problems involving the four operations, and identify and explain patterns in arithmetic.
Lesson 2.6	3.OA.D Solve problems involving the four operations, and identify and explain patterns in arithmetic.
Lesson 3.1	3.NF.A Develop understanding of fractions as numbers.
Lesson 3.2	3.NF.A Develop understanding of fractions as numbers.
Lesson 3.3	3.NF.A Develop understanding of fractions as numbers.
Lesson 4.1	3.MD.A Solve problems involving measurement and estimation.
Lesson 4.2	3.MD.A Solve problems involving measurement and estimation.
Lesson 4.3	3.MD.B Represent and interpret data.
Lesson 4.4	3.MD.B Represent and interpret data.

Lesson	Common Core State Standards
Lesson 4.5	3.MD.C Geometric measurement: understand concepts of area and relate area to multiplication and to addition.
Lesson 4.6	3.MD.C Geometric measurement: understand concepts of area and relate area to multiplication and to addition.
Lesson 4.7	3.MD.C Geometric measurement: understand concepts of area and relate area to multiplication and to addition.
Lesson 4.8	3.MD.D Geometric measurement: recognize perimeter.
Lesson 5.1	3.G.A Reason with shapes and their attributes.
Lesson 5.2	3.G.A Reason with shapes and their attributes.